NEW DIRECTIONS FOR STUDENT SERVICES

John H. Schuh, *Iowa State University*
EDITOR-IN-CHIEF

Elizabeth J. Whitt, *University of Iowa*
ASSOCIATE EDITOR

Responding to the New Affirmative Action Climate

Donald D. Gehring
Bowling Green State University

EDITOR

Number 83, Fall 1998

JOSSEY-BASS PUBLISHERS
San Francisco

RESPONDING TO THE NEW AFFIRMATIVE ACTION CLIMATE
Donald D. Gehring (ed.)
New Directions for Student Services, no. 83
John H. Schuh, Editor-in-Chief
Elizabeth J. Whitt, Associate Editor

Microfilm copies of issues and articles are available in 16mm and 35mm, as well as microfiche in 105mm, through University Microfilms Inc., 300 North Zeeb Road, Ann Arbor, Michigan 48106–1346.

ISSN 0164-7970   ISBN 0-7879-4215-4

NEW DIRECTIONS FOR STUDENT SERVICES is part of The Jossey-Bass Higher and Adult Education Series and is published quarterly by Jossey-Bass Inc., Publishers, 350 Sansome Street, San Francisco, California 94104–1342. Periodicals postage paid at San Francisco, California, and at additional mailing offices. Postmaster: Send address changes to New Directions for Student Services, Jossey-Bass Inc., Publishers, 350 Sansome Street, San Francisco, California 94104–1342.

New Directions for Student Services® is indexed in College Student Personnel Abstracts and Contents Pages in Education.

SUBSCRIPTIONS cost $56.00 for individuals and $99.00 for institutions, agencies, and libraries. See ordering information page at end of book.

EDITORIAL CORRESPONDENCE should be sent to the Editor-in-Chief, John H. Schuh, Campus Box 8, Wichita State University, Wichita, Kansas 67260-0008.

Cover photograph by Wernher Krutein/PHOTOVAULT © 1990.

Jossey-Bass Web address: www.josseybass.com

Printed in the United States of America on acid-free recycled paper containing 100 percent recovered waste paper, of which at least 20 percent is postconsumer waste.

CONTENTS

EDITOR'S NOTES

The term *affirmative action* stirs hot debate wherever it is mentioned. The issue has been contested vehemently in state legislatures and courts throughout the nation, yet there is still a lack of common understanding about what the concept really means and how it should be put into practice, if at all. The term carries a lot of baggage, such as preferences, quotas, reverse discrimination, and set-asides, and there is a reluctance on the part of some professionals even to discuss the issue for fear of being labeled racist. Some see affirmative action as the only way to prepare students for the diverse world they will face; others view it as an unlawful and irrational basis for discussions about admissions, financial aid, and employment. Even the courts are divided and have sent confusing and conflicting messages, making it difficult for administrators of higher education to understand the parameters of the law. The Supreme Court has done little in recent years to clarify the legal boundaries of affirmative action in higher education.

Although the term *affirmative action* may push our buttons as a nation, almost everyone in higher education would agree that students learn a great deal from one another, and that a diverse student body is a positive educational environment. An expression of one of my graduate professors that I have found most useful throughout my own career is, "We all exist in a state of relative ignorance." What he meant is, we all know things that others do not, and others know things that we do not. Thus we have much to learn from one another. A socially, economically, ethnically, spiritually, culturally, and otherwise diverse student body can have a significant impact on the free marketplace of ideas that is higher education. The problem we face is how to achieve that educational goal while complying with confusing and conflicting laws and judicial pronouncements.

The purpose of this issue of *New Directions for Student Services* is to assist all higher education leaders who want to create diverse, educationally beneficial environments for learning. It is not intended to end the debate; in fact, one chapter challenges the narrow concept of affirmative action by suggesting a broader view. Only by civil and informed debate can we come to a common understanding as well as to the best possible solution for ways to diversify our institutions and enhance student learning within the parameters of the law.

The volume begins by providing a brief historical overview of affirmative action. Both the social and legal arguments surrounding affirmative action are provided to help the reader understand how affirmative action evolved from the days of Booker T. Washington and W.E.B. DuBois to the modern era of the Civil Rights Act. Robert D. Bickel pulls together the legal and social implications of a policy of "inclusion" and argues for a reconceptualization of standards.

In Chapter Two, Alan T. Kolling clarifies the law as it relates to affirmative action in admissions and financial aid. The chapter identifies the parameters of the law as currently applied to higher education. Kolling explains with precision how the law has evolved in the federal system as well as the current standards used by the courts to evaluate the legality of affirmative action in admissions and financial aid programs. The chapter also provides insight into California's Proposition 209.

The affirmative action debate continues in Chapter Three, in which Gary Pavela asks, "What's Wrong with 'Race-Based' Affirmative Action?" Picking up on California's Proposition 209, Pavela examines the question of race-based remedies not only for higher education but also as national social policy. He then suggests that a commitment to true diversity must include a caste approach and diversity of opinion. The chapter concludes with a dialogue between Pavela and legal scholar Bill Kaplin about the *Bakke* decision, including a reexamination of Justice Powell's opinion.

In Chapter Four, Carol Logan Patitu and Melvin C. Terrell examine a variety of affirmative action programs that have been diversifying campuses throughout the country. The authors report on a national study of student affairs programs that have been shown to benefit students and the larger university community through the use of affirmative action. These programs provide higher education leaders with a picture of what is possible and an appreciation of the benefits of affirmative action.

The judicial mandate to eliminate an affirmative action admissions program in Texas has had a significant effect on many areas in student affairs. Felicia J. Scott and William L. Kibler, both student affairs practitioners in Texas, discuss the chronology of the *Hopwood* decision and how institutions have responded to the issues raised by the decision.

In the concluding chapter, Bettina C. Shuford looks beyond the current controversy and asks what could be possible if affirmative action as we know it today were to be scrapped by the Supreme Court or state legislatures. She brings the volume full circle by suggesting alternatives based on Bickel's proposition in Chapter One, that what constitutes merit should be reconceptualized. Shuford's practical suggestions for student affairs professionals offer concrete ways to enhance campus diversity by taking affirmative actions.

The ideas and concepts in this volume are offered for thoughtful consideration and reflection. The authors, a multiethnic group, have provided a variety of perspectives on ways to create a diverse campus community so that higher education may truly be a marketplace of ideas in which students are prepared to think, learn, and grow in a changing world. The very survival of our society depends upon creating this environment.

Donald D. Gehring
Editor

DONALD D. GEHRING is professor of higher education and student affairs and director of the higher education doctoral program at Bowling Green State University.

Affirmative action was called for long before President Kennedy signed his executive order. This chapter explores the roots of current affirmative action arguments.

A Brief History of the Commitment to Inclusion as a Facet of Equal Educational Opportunity

Robert D. Bickel

It may be said that the popular debate about equal educational opportunity began with the 1903 response of W.E.B. DuBois to Booker T. Washington's program of industrial education for the Negro. Referring illustratively to the intellectual brilliance of Benjamin Banneker and to Frederick Douglass's ideal of ultimate assimilation through self-assertion, DuBois respectfully rejected Mr. Washington's compromise of political power, civil rights, and higher education for the Negro as a means of gaining popular commitment to the Negro's economic advancement. In *The Souls of Black Folk* ([1903] 1989), DuBois wrote that the legacy of Washington's "Atlanta Compromise" included the disfranchisement of the Negro, the legal creation of civil inferiority, and an actual withdrawal of aid from institutions for the higher training of the Negro. DuBois gave voice to the respectful demand that the Negro enjoy the right to vote and civic equality, and that Negro youth be educated according to ability.

DuBois was typical of black scholars who had been subjected to a policy of segregation in higher education. He graduated from Fisk University in Nashville, one of a very few universities (including Shaw University in Raleigh, N.C., and Morehouse College in Atlanta) established to provide a liberal arts education for young black scholars, and earned three degrees at Harvard University, graduating with a Ph.D. in 1895. The modern history of the higher education of black citizens certainly identifies DuBois as a leader of the movement to advance the presence of black faculty in historically white universities and to provide a true university education for black students (Fleming, Gill, and Swinton, 1978).

NEW DIRECTIONS FOR STUDENT SERVICES, no. 83, Fall 1998 © Jossey-Bass Publishers

A related perspective on the history of the concept we have come to call affirmative action can be traced to John Stuart Mill's essay *On Liberty* ([1859] 1978). In Chapter Two, Mill writes of the advantage of diversity of opinion in a society seeking intellectual advancement. His famous argument that popular opinions must be submitted to the marketplace of ideas is timeless in reminding us that even the most commonly accepted perceptions of a society are not necessarily truths. Perceptions are narrowed by the limits or biases of experience, education, geography, or class, so when they become the basis of judgment and social policy, true social advancement is compromised. DuBois sought nothing more than a formal commitment to including the Negro in those social institutions that most effectively promote intellectual advancement, moral argument, and social view.

The Black Colleges and Universities and Black Scholars

Between World Wars I and II and even after World War II, black students and faculty studied and taught, for the most part, at black colleges and universities that were challenged by lack of state and federal funding, poor library facilities, inadequate laboratory equipment, and insufficient teacher preparation. Except for Fisk, Xavier, Howard, and Atlanta Universities, and Hampton Institute, virtually no black colleges offered graduate or professional education. White universities did begin to admit black graduate students in larger numbers in the 1930s, but by 1942 blacks constituted substantially less than 1 percent of graduates receiving Ph.D. degrees, and most of these recipients were trained in black undergraduate colleges. The experience of black faculty was similar, and with few exceptions even pioneers in research, such as Charles Drew and Percy Julian, spent their careers at black universities (Fleming, Gill, and Swinton, 1978).

Desegregation of Public Schools and the Civil Rights Movement

The first major step toward inclusion in education was the abatement of segregation in the nation's public schools, beginning with the cases of Harry Briggs Jr., Ethel Belton, Dorothy Davis, and Linda Brown. Out of these consolidated cases came the Supreme Court's ruling on May 17, 1954, in *Brown v. Board of Education of Topeka* (1954) that the segregation of public schools as a form of racial isolation had a damaging effect on black children. The testimony in *Brown* included that of Horace B. English, a professor of psychology at Ohio State University, who asserted that if we persistently tell a person that it is unnatural for him to learn certain things, or that he is incapable of learning, then he is less likely to learn (Williams, 1987, p. 24). Supreme Court Justice Thurgood Marshall incorporated this testimony in an appendix to his brief in the Briggs case and argued that the only way a state could attempt to justify the segregation of black school children was to claim that Negroes were different from everybody else.

The essence of the Supreme Court's opinion in *Brown* (the consolidated cases) pronounced that the segregation of children in public schools solely because of their race generates in those children a feeling of inferiority as to their status in the community that may affect their hearts and minds in a way that is very unlikely ever to be undone. Thus the Court held that separate schools, even if equal in tangible factors, are inherently unequal (Williams, 1987).

Despite the voluntary admission of black students to schools such as the law school of the University of Arkansas, Fayetteville, as early as 1948, resistance to *Brown* in the South was rapid and politically charged. Formal legal efforts to prevent black students from attending Central High School in Little Rock, Arkansas, and threats to their safety posed by mobs of segregationist white citizens, led to President Dwight Eisenhower's ordering of federal troops to Little Rock in September 1957 to escort Central High's first black students to school. This resistance—in Arkansas, Georgia, and elsewhere—continued into the 1960s, an era marked by the demand of segregationist governors that blacks not be enrolled in publicly supported white universities. Higher education's version of Central High School was the University of Mississippi, where riots occurred in 1962 as James Meredith enrolled as the university's first black student, pursuant to the order of a federal district court.

Out of this resistance to the integration of public schools and universities came the modern civil rights movement, calling for equal educational opportunity, equal employment opportunity, voting rights, and nondiscrimination in housing. The movement began in Montgomery, Alabama, in the fall of 1955 as a protest of the segregation of seating on city buses. It achieved popular and political prominence in Nashville, Tennessee; Albany and Atlanta, Georgia; and Birmingham, Alabama in the demand for desegregation of lunch counters and interstate transportation. The movement mobilized the efforts of thousands of black and white citizens throughout the South (as well as northern white citizens, students, and lawyers) to bring about federal judicial and legislative mandates for civic equality and economic and educational opportunity for black citizens. Stephen Halpern (1995) writes that the movement's commitment to nonviolence and its identity as a Christian movement, organized and led by black clergy, created public sympathy for its goals, particularly in the North. Halpern emphasizes, however, that it was white resistance, characterized by savage police methods, church bombings, and the murders of civil rights workers, that galvanized popular support for social change. The hundreds of demonstrations in cities throughout the South and the hundreds of racial disturbances of the summer of 1963 culminated in the August 1963 march on Washington, attended by more than 250,000 people supporting the enactment of federal civil rights legislation. The demands of the movement's leaders, and the exigency created by southern violence toward the movement, led to the enactment of the Civil Rights Act of 1964, and the Voting Rights Act of 1965 (Halpern, 1995).

Title VI of the Civil Rights Act of 1964

The legal path toward inclusion in higher education, which began with the constitutional pronouncements in *Brown,* is marked most prominently by the enactment of Title VI of the Civil Rights Act (42 U.S.C., § 2000d) and the Supreme Court's decision in *Regents of the University of California* v. *Bakke* (1978).

Title VI was enacted to enforce, among other things, the desegregation of public elementary, secondary, and postsecondary educational institutions by assuring that federal financial assistance would not be allocated to education programs unless those programs provided equal educational opportunity without regard to race. As with Title VII of the Civil Rights Act, however, which provided for equal employment opportunity (42 U.S.C., § 2000e), Title VI was aimed at ensuring nondiscrimination while making no demand for voluntary efforts to create significant representation of minorities in proportion to their presence in the community. Because the culture of the time remained tainted by significant popular sympathy for segregation, the legislative history of both sections of the statute includes a record eighty-three-day debate and significant formal opposition to preferences based on race or efforts to achieve racial balance. Indeed, Senate approval for mere nondiscrimination based on race passed with twenty-seven dissenting votes (Celada, 1965).

Despite the Supreme Court's pronouncements in *Brown,* virtually all black children in the former Confederate states attended segregated schools in 1963. Of the 4,094 school districts in the southern and border states in 1964, more than half, enrolling more than three million black children, remained fully segregated. By April 1965, when the Department of Health, Education, and Welfare (HEW) began enforcing Title VI, only 142 of the nation's 27,000 school districts had been desegregated by court order (Halpern, 1995; "U.S. Bids Schools End Segregation by Fall of 1967," 1965, p. 1). In response to this lack of progress, HEW proposed guidelines imposing numerical goals that focused on the percentage of black children who should be enrolled in previously all-white schools. In *United States* v. *Jefferson County Board of Education* (1967), the U.S. Court of Appeals for the Fifth Circuit endorsed this approach to achieving racial integration, holding that HEW had the authority to impose on school boards an affirmative duty to integrate. Implementing legislation, most notably the Elementary and Secondary Education Act of 1965, provided school districts with federal monies for speeding up integration by funding special education programs for disadvantaged children (Halpern, 1995).

Title VI and Higher Education

Higher Education became the subject of similar demands for integration in *Adams* v. *Richardson* (1973), a case charging that HEW was lagging in its efforts to enforce Title VI following the election of Richard Nixon as president. Although HEW had sought desegregation plans from ten states that had operated dual systems of higher education (historically black colleges and white colleges that barred blacks), it had delayed formal action to approve or reject such plans. The Court of Appeals criticized HEW's reliance on voluntary compliance but held that desegregation problems in higher education were different from those in elementary and secondary education, particularly with regard to the role of historically black colleges in training minority professionals. This issue became significant when guidelines proffered by the plaintiff's lawyers in the *Adams* case and embraced by Peter Holmes, director of the Office of Civil Rights, sought specific responses from certain southern states as to the impact of academic decisions on future segregation, the allocation of resources and educational roles assigned to black and white colleges and universities, the duplication of programs, student recruitment, the retention of black students, and programs for desegregating faculties and staffs and for increasing the number of black faculty. To the extent that the ultimate goal of the desegregation of higher education was to increase the number of black lawyers, doctors, engineers, and other professionals, the demand for increased enrollment of black students at previously all-white colleges subsumed a concern for the special problems of the historically black colleges that in the past had provided access to higher education for blacks. While recognizing this concern, and making some provision for the vitality of historically black colleges, HEW issued guidelines (within the context of the *Adams* litigation) mandating a unitary system of higher education, free of the vestiges of the historical dual system operated under racial segregation. Affirmative action requirements included adoption of the goal that the proportion of black high school graduates entering state institutions of higher education should equal the proportion of white high school graduates entering such institutions, including graduate and professional schools; allocation of financial aid; and implementation of remedial education programs to reduce the disparity between the graduation rates of whites and blacks. Halpern (1995, p. 180) cites the observation of a southern black leader at the time, that what "is at issue . . . is the development of another class of educated people. . . . Even though a lot of black students who will be admitted to these institutions will not be able to maximize [opportunities] because of their own disadvantaged backgrounds, perhaps 25 percent will. So we're talking . . . about a million people going to college . . . in the south who would not normally have been there in the past. And . . . 250,000 of them will enter the 'system.' Then there will be consequences that will flow from their new positions and from what they, in turn, will be able to give to their children and their children's children."

Title VII: Equal Employment Opportunity and Affirmative Action

The passage of Title VII of the Civil Rights Act, which sought to end discrimination against blacks in employment, was accompanied by presidential mandates for affirmative action as we have come to define the term. In the spirit of former President Franklin D. Roosevelt's executive order that Negroes be accepted into job training programs in the 1940s, Presidents Kennedy and Johnson issued Executive Orders 10925, 11246, and 11375, which created the Presidential Commission on Equal Employment Opportunity and ordered contractors doing business with the federal government to end discrimination in jobs and take positive steps to redress the absence of minorities in the workforce resulting from past societal discrimination. Title VII itself, in requiring an end to job discrimination on the basis of race, ethnicity, sex, and religion, afforded federal courts the power to require the hiring of minorities as a remedial measure when an employer was proven to have discriminated in hiring, promotion, or retention on the basis of race or other protected traits. (This authority continues to be an accepted form of affirmative action.) The executive orders also addressed, however, the broader current effects of past societal discrimination and gave a larger meaning to the term *affirmative action*.

President Johnson justified the executive orders by observing that merely ending overt discrimination would not in itself overcome the effect of years of systematic exclusion of blacks from jobs and education. Recruitment, hiring, and promotion of blacks were also required. President Nixon reaffirmed and extended the actions of the Kennedy and Johnson administrations by unveiling the "Philadelphia Plan" for bringing minorities into formerly segregated trades, and by issuing Revised Executive Order No. 4, which required annual affirmative action plans, including hiring goals and timetables, from major contractors (Urofsky, 1991).

Title VII seemed to move beyond federally mandated affirmative action requiring federally supported contractors to create jobs for minorities by permitting private employers to engage in voluntary programs to expand jobs and job training programs for minorities. In *United Steelworkers of America* v. *Weber* (1979), the Supreme Court allowed a private employer to adopt a voluntary affirmative action plan calling for hiring ratios based on a conspicuous racial imbalance in traditionally segregated job categories, even though such affirmative action could not be ordered by a court in the absence of a finding of persistent or egregious discrimination. And in *Johnson* v. *Transportation Agency, Santa Clara County* (1987), the Court held that while an affirmative action plan should not require the hiring of an unqualified applicant, such a plan may allow a private or public employer to consider race or sex as a factor in the hiring of qualified applicants to remedy a conspicuous absence of women or minorities in the employer's workforce (Player, 1988).

Admissions Quotas Versus Consideration of Race or Ethnicity in Admissions: The *Bakke* Case

Regents of the University of California v. *Bakke* (1978) is considered the seminal affirmative action case in higher education. In *Bakke*, the Supreme Court reconsidered, in a different light, Justice John Harlan's observation in his dissenting opinion in *Plessy* v. *Ferguson* (1896) that "[in] view of the Constitution, in the eye of the law, there is in this country no superior, dominant, ruling class of citizens. There is no caste here. Our Constitution is colorblind, and neither knows nor tolerates classes among citizens" (p. 559). The *Bakke* case placed before the Supreme Court, for the first time, the consequences of the historical exclusion of black citizens from white universities throughout the country, and the resistance from 1965 into the 1970s of judicial efforts to abate the structural dual systems of higher education perpetuated by predominantly white and predominantly black colleges.

Allan Bakke's lawsuit essentially challenged, under the Fourteenth Amendment and Title VI of the Civil Rights Act, the decision of the University of California–Davis Medical School to redress voluntarily the historical exclusion of blacks from white medical colleges by reserving sixteen seats in its entering class for economically disadvantaged African Americans, Chicanos, Asians, and Native Americans. This policy of providing educational and professional opportunities for underrepresented or traditionally subordinated groups came to be described as a form of voluntary affirmative action. Bakke alleged that the granting of this "preference" to minorities constituted a form of discrimination that was illegal under Title VI and the Constitution, even if it was benign and remedial in nature.

The Court had spoken early in its history, in *Sweatt* v. *Painter* (1950), against segregation in higher education, observing that a law school cannot be effective in isolation from the individuals with whom the law interacts. The Court, however, had not ruled on the issue of whether an institution of higher education could work toward inclusion by voluntarily encouraging the rapid admission of groups historically excluded by dual systems of public higher education.

The University of California defended its special admissions program by arguing that the program served compelling state interests in reducing the historic deficit of minorities in medical schools and the profession, remedying the effects of societal discrimination, increasing the number of physicians who will practice in areas traditionally understaffed, and obtaining the educational benefits that flow from a culturally diverse student body. In what one writer has called one of the most narrowly decided decisions in history, the Court invalidated the set-aside feature of the UC–Davis admissions program but approved the consideration of race and ethnic origin as a factor in the admissions process (Ward, 1991). The *Bakke* court was significantly divided on the issue of the constitutionality of a benign preference for minorities in admissions and did not deliver a majority opinion. In the end, a majority of the justices found that the state's concern for reducing the historic deficit of minorities in medical schools and the profession, and for remedying the effects of societal discrimination, was insufficient to justify a race-exclusive admissions process. A majority of the Court did hold, however, that the First-Amendment interest in academic freedom, evidenced by the university's concern that it admit a culturally diverse student body, constituted a compelling state interest under the Fourteenth Amendment's equal protection clause.

Justice Lewis Powell, in an opinion that is seen as central to the Court's rationale, observed that a diverse student body contributes to a robust exchange of ideas that is necessary to the intellectual life of the university. The atmosphere of "speculation, experiment, and creation" that is so essential to the quality of higher education, Justice Powell wrote, is widely believed to be promoted by a diverse student body. He cautioned, however, that the state's interest in preserving this marketplace of ideas "is not an interest in simple ethnic diversity, in which a specified percentage of the student body is in effect guaranteed to be members of selected ethnic groups, with the remaining percentage an undifferentiated aggregation of students. The diversity that furthers a compelling state interest encompasses a far broader array of qualifications and characteristics of which racial or ethnic origin is but a single though important interest" (*Regents of the University of California* v. *Bakke,* 1978, pp. 312–315). This observation led to Justice Powell's famous statement in the same case that, although race or ethnicity should not demand inclusion or exclusion, minority racial or ethnic status could constitute a "plus" in an applicant's admissions file. Four justices (William Brennan, Byron White, Thurgood Marshall, and Harry Blackmun) dissented from the disapproval of the UC–Davis admissions process, reasoning that the effects of past societal discrimination in public education, including higher education, produced an underrepresentation of minorities in higher education that was both substantial and chronic and impeded access of minorities to medical school. Moreover, these justices found that the special admissions program was appropriate where the university could not practically achieve its objectives without the use of race-conscious measures. They implied that it is beyond cavil that whites as a group are not burdened with the disabilities associated with minority status because they have not been subjected to purposeful unequal treatment on account of race or relegated to such a position of political powerlessness as to require extraordinary protections from the majoritarian political process.

Although Justice Powell's opinion in *Bakke* is most often referenced as establishing the parameters of what has come to be known as affirmative action in admissions, it is Justice Blackmun who may have captured the moral justification for affirmative action. Justice Blackmun wrote, in words both forthright and powerful, that "[in] order to get beyond racism we must first take account of race. There is no other way. And in order to treat some persons equally, we must first treat them differently" (*Regents of the University of California* v. *Bakke,* 1978, p. 407). Justice Blackmun's willingness to unmask the undeniable racism that existed in American higher education into the 1970s challenged the Court to recognize the *moral* argument for affirmative action.

The legacy of *Bakke* is profound, and disturbing. Although the Court reached its decision by the narrowest of votes, lower federal courts have relied on *Bakke* in striking down any form of inclusion that ensures the admission of a culturally diverse student body by treating minority students differently from white students in the admissions process. The historical objective of affirmative action programs in higher education has been to select students who

demonstrate potential for success in college-level work but who do not necessarily meet all the traditional admissions requirements of the college (Scanlan,
1996). In keeping with this purpose, the "Harvard Plan," which allowed
minority racial or ethnic origin to be a plus in the admissions process, was
clearly approved in *Bakke*. The competitive nature of college admissions, however, and the refusal of most universities to depart from the use of grades and
entrance test scores as virtually dispositive screening devices, impedes significantly the inclusion of minority students in the culture of the American college or university.

The essential philosophical observation of the Supreme Court's seminal
decision in *Bakke* is that there is an inevitable and necessary relationship
between cultural diversity and intellectual diversity. When we are surrounded
by people who think as we do, our perceptions become our truths, without
the benefit of the perspective of persons raised in cultural contexts that espouse
other ideas. Nowhere is this more evident than in the multicultural history of
the United States, which is now reconstructing the traditional history that we
were taught (Takaki, 1993).

Stated pragmatically, diversity includes a civic component (harkening to
DuBois's call for civic equality) that furthers the interest of society in producing educated individuals, including future business and political leaders, who
have been exposed to a wide variety of viewpoints and who are themselves rich
in diverse experiences. This goal, it is argued, cannot be achieved without a
fair and reasonable representation of all viewpoints among a student body, and
the views of groups that have been the victims of discrimination are unlikely,
in the absence of affirmative action, to be fully represented in higher education programs that train public and corporate leaders (Scanlan, 1996).

The remedial objective of affirmative action in higher education sought to
remedy the effects of formal, societal discrimination against minorities characterized by the perpetuation of structural and *de facto* dual systems of higher
education into the 1970s. Proponents of the remedial objective argue that certain classes of minority students who are especially burdened by this dual system do in fact suffer the vestiges of that discrimination in that they cannot
fairly compete for admission to selective colleges and universities on the basis
of criteria traditionally defined by a favored or privileged class. As Laura Scanlan (1996) observes, such vestiges of discrimination include the current ten-
dency of schools to have low expectations of minority students, which
influences their placement in low-ability classes. Affirmative action viewed in
this context encompasses both compensatory and distributive justice goals.

The Connection Between Law and Educational Policy

The educational debate about inclusion in higher education has given way to
a legal debate about the balancing of individual rights and group rights, including distributive justice. Although philosophical and moral arguments strongly
support concerns for group rights in the context of educational opportunity,

legal arguments that rest on the equal protection clause and federal legislation balance compensation for past injustices against the protection of the individual rights of those who are, by traditional measures, more qualified for admission to college. Thus the race-conscious selection of minority students on the basis of a two-track or special admissions process that makes race or ethnicity a dispositive factor in the admission of the student is viewed as "reverse discrimination" against a white student with better undergraduate grades and test scores.

The reverse discrimination argument has succeeded. As is explained in the following chapters, although colleges and universities have sought through affirmative action policies to admit the most diverse possible group of students with high intelligence and character, many such colleges have deliberately lowered traditional admissions criteria for minority candidates rather than reconstruct admissions criteria for all candidates. This establishment of race-based admission quotas, rather than goals that inspire educationally sound reconceptualizations of admissions criteria and expanded recruiting of students, arguably compromises both the equal protection clause and Title VI of the Civil Rights Act (Urofsky, 1991).

Even more important to the historical goals of affirmative action, courts that accepted the arguments of educators about segregation have disagreed with proinclusion educators on the question of whether minority students suffer a present effect of past discrimination, and whether cultural diversity is necessary to achieve intellectual diversity. Despite the observations of writers like Daniel Maguire (1992) that some form of temporary unequal treatment is justified by our concern for the inclusion of African American, Latino, and other students in numbers that accelerate their representation in the national workforce, critics argue that discrimination on the basis of race, in any form, violates the law, unless it seeks to remedy identifiable current discrimination in admissions (Maguire, 1992; Maguire, 1977). Moreover, sociologists and educators continue to debate whether placing students of color in integrated classrooms or extracurricular environments will guarantee equal educational opportunity (Halpern, 1995). The following chapters examine the extent to which legal doctrine and educational philosophy support the notion that the cultural diversity of a university's student body contributes to intellectual diversity in ways that benefit students in all facets of the university experience.

Court Cases Cited

Adams v. Richardson, 358 F.Supp. 97 (D.D.C., 1973), 480 F.2d 1163 (D.C.Cir, 1973) en banc.

Briggs et al. v. Elliott et al., 98 F.Supp. 529 (E.D.S.C. 1951), 103 F. Supp. 920 (E.D.S.C. 1952).

Brown v. Board of Education of Topeka, 347 U.S. 493 (1954).

Executive Order No. 11246, 3 C.F.R. 339 (1964-1965).

Executive Order No. 11375, 3 C.F.R. 684 (1966-1970).

Johnson v. Transportation Agency, Santa Clara County, 480 U.S. 616 (1987).

Plessy v. *Ferguson,* 163 U.S. 537 (1896).
Regents of the University of California v. *Bakke,* 438 U.S. 265 (1978).
Revised Executive Order No. 4, 41 C.F.R., Part 60-2 (1997).
Sweatt v. *Painter,* 339 U.S. 629 (1950).
United States v. *Jefferson County Board of Education,* 372 F.2d 836, 380 F.2d 385 (5th Cir. 1967).
United Steelworkers of America v. *Weber,* 443 U.S. 193 (1979).

References

Celada, R. "Nondiscrimination in Federally Assisted Programs: Legislative History and Analysis of Title VI of the Civil Rights Act of 1964." Washington, D.C.: Library of Congress, 1965.

DuBois, W.E.B. *The Souls of Black Folk.* New York: Penguin Books, 1989. (Originally published 1903.)

Fleming, J., Gill, G., and Swinton, D. *The Case for Affirmative Action for Blacks in Higher Education.* Washington, D.C.: Howard University Press, 1978.

Halpern, S. "On the Limits of the Law: The Ironic Legacy of Title VI of the 1964 Civil Rights Act." Baltimore: The Johns Hopkins University Press, 1995.

Maguire, D. "Unequal But Fair: The Morality of Justice by Quota." *Commonweal,* 1977, *104.*

Maguire, D. *A Case for Affirmative Action.* Dubuque, Iowa: Sheperds Publishing, 1992.

Player, M. *Employment Discrimination Law.* St. Paul, Minn.: West, 1988.

Mill, J. S. *On Liberty.* Indianapolis, Ind.: Hackett, 1978. (Originally published 1859.)

Scanlan, L. "*Hopwood* v. *Texas:* A Backward Look at Affirmative Action in Education." *New York University Law Review,* 1996, *71,* 1580.

Takaki, R. "A Different Mirror: A History of Multicultural America." New York: Little, Brown, 1993.

Urofsky, M. "A Conflict of Rights: The Supreme Court and Affirmative Action." New York: Scribner, 1991.

"U.S. Bids Schools End Segregation by Fall of 1967." *New York Times,* April 30, 1965.

Ward, J. "Race-Exclusive Scholarships: Do They Violate the Constitution and Title VI of the Civil Rights Act of 1964?" *Journal of College and University Law,* 1991, *18,* 73.

Williams, J. *Eyes on the Prize.* New York: Penguin Books, 1987.

ROBERT BICKEL *is professor of law at Stetson University College of Law.*

*This chapter reviews developments in the law regarding student
affirmative action in college admissions and financial aid, and reflects
on the growing trend toward state referenda banning preferences based
on race and gender.*

Student Affirmative Action and the Courts

Alan T. Kolling

Recent court decisions and the passage of California's statewide Proposition
209 have fueled the national debate over the continuing use of voluntary affirmative action programs in higher education, resulting in a major reexamination of admissions and financial aid programs by colleges and universities
around the country. To date, only two cases involving student affirmative
action issues, *DeFunis v. Odegaard* (1974) and *Regents of the University of California v. Bakke* (1978), have been reviewed by the U.S. Supreme Court, with
the multiple opinions in the *Bakke* decision providing limited insight and
guidance into the validity of current affirmative action programs in postsecondary education.

Historically, the concept of affirmative action was born out of President
Kennedy's 1961 executive order calling for government contractors to under-
take affirmative action voluntarily to recruit minorities and to encourage their
hiring and promotion. But affirmative action efforts were not always voluntarily undertaken. The subsequent passage of the Civil Rights Act of 1964
and the Education Amendments Act of 1972 provided the statutory bases for
enforcing the ban on race and gender-based discrimination in all programs
receiving federal funds, including public and private educational institutions.
Acting pursuant to the Civil Rights Act, the U.S. Department of Health, Education, and Welfare (HEW), through its Office of Civil Rights (OCR), sought
and obtained judicial orders in *Adams v. Richardson* (1973) requiring ten
states (Louisiana, Mississippi, Oklahoma, North Carolina, Florida, Arkansas,

The author wishes to thank Raymond H. Goldstone for his assistance and time in writing
this chapter.

Pennsylvania, Georgia, Maryland, and Virginia) to abandon their racially separate higher education systems, which had been in existence for many years.

As part of the court-approved desegregation plans, OCR insisted on the states' adoption of specific remedial measures in college admissions and financial aid practices. Many of these remedial measures were later adopted by other educational institutions around the country. Although most of adoptions were on a voluntary basis, that is, in the absence of a specific court order or administrative enforcement proceeding, the concerted efforts by OCR to dismantle racially segregated education systems in the South clearly influenced institutions in other parts of the country to adopt similar measures as a precaution against such federal intervention. Ironically, many of the remedial measures voluntarily adopted pursuant to the implementation of the court-approved desegregation plans are now under direct legal attack (White, 1996, p. 5).

In light of the Supreme Court's failure to review any student affirmative action cases since the *Bakke* decision, this chapter reviews the conflicting lower court decisions dealing with voluntary affirmative action efforts, considers general guidelines that administrators may wish to consider in devising their policies and programs, and reflects on the growing trend toward resolving the debate through the passage of state referenda banning the use of race or gender preferences.

DeFunis: An Early Challenge

The first judicial challenge to the use of affirmative action in higher education admissions occurred in *DeFunis* v. *Odegaard* (1973), where on appeal the Washington State Supreme Court overturned the trial court's finding that the University of Washington Law School's minority admissions program was unconstitutional. At issue was the law school's practice of considering minority applications separately from other applications and attaching less importance to minority applicants' so-called "predicted first-year averages," a numerical index combining the undergraduate grade point average and the LSAT score. DeFunis was a white male applicant who argued that less qualified minority applicants had been accepted under the affirmative action program.

The Washington State Supreme Court upheld the law school's admissions practices because of the compelling state interests that it found were served by the program. Among these were the "interest in promoting integration in public education," the educational interest "in producing a racially balanced student body at the law school," and the interest in alleviating "the shortage of minority attorneys—and consequently, minority prosecutors, judges, and public officials" (pp. 1182–1184). DeFunis, however, was allowed to remain in the University of Washington law school while he sought further review of his case.

The U.S. Supreme Court, with four justices dissenting, subsequently dismissed the case on the grounds of mootness because DeFunis was about to graduate and the law school had taken the position that it would not alter his registration regardless of the outcome of the case. Although concluding that the case was moot, the U.S. Supreme Court took the unusual step of vacating the Washington State Supreme Court's decision and remanding the case "for such proceedings as by that court may be deemed appropriate" (p. 320). On remand, the Washington State Supreme Court reinstated and reaffirmed its earlier decision, upholding the constitutionality of the use of race as a factor in admissions.

In his dissent, Justice William Douglas of the U.S. Supreme Court took issue with the preference granted to applicants on the basis of race, although he recognized that the preference "was not absolute." He noted that the law school "did accord all such applicants a preference, by applying, to an extent not precisely ascertainable from the record, different standards by which to judge their applications, with the result that the committee admitted minority applicants who, in the school's own judgment, were less promising than other applicants who were rejected. Furthermore, it is apparent that because the admissions committee compared minority applicants only with one another, it was necessary to reserve some proportion of the class for them, even if at the outset a precise number of places were not set aside" (*DeFunis v. Odegaard*, 1973, p. 332). Justice Douglas thus would have preferred to see the law school adopt an affirmative action program that focused on "an applicant's prior achievements in light of the barriers that he had to overcome." Citing examples of how such a background could apply to "a poor Appalachian white, or a second-generation Chinese in San Francisco, or some other American whose lineage is so diverse as to defy ethnic labels," Justice Douglas remarked that "the difference between such a policy and the one presented in [*DeFunis*] is that the committee would be making decisions on the basis of individual attributes, rather than according a preference solely on the basis of race" (pp. 332–333).

As one commentator noted, "Justice Douglas did not conclude that the university's policy was therefore unconstitutional but, rather, that it would be unconstitutional unless, after a new trial, the court found that it took account of 'cultural standards of a diverse rather than homogeneous society' in a 'racially neutral' way" (Kaplin and Lee, 1995, p. 403). The two notions advanced in Justice Douglas's dissent, that the diversity of the entering class should not be strictly defined along racial or ethnic lines and that individual comparisons among applicants across the board should always be made, foreshadowed the key principles that would emerge from later cases dealing with student affirmative action.

The *Bakke* Opinions

In *Regents of the University of California v. Bakke* (1978), the Supreme Court finally confronted the legal dilemmas involved in a university admissions program, but the decision that emerged provided less than a clear ruling on the troubling affirmative action issues that were presented.

Bakke posed a challenge to the use of a separate admissions process, including a separate admissions committee composed primarily of members of minority groups, for minority admissions at the University of California at Davis's Medical School. The school had reserved sixteen places out of one hundred for disadvantaged members of certain minority groups, offering the following four justifications for the special admissions program:

- The need to reduce the historic deficit of minorities in the medical schools and profession
- The need to counter the effects of societal discrimination against members of minority groups
- The need to increase the number of physicians who would practice in underserved minority communities
- The need to foster an ethnically diverse student body and to derive the educational benefits that flowed from that process

Transferring the case directly from the trial court without intermediate appellate court review because of the importance of the issue, the California State Supreme Court held that the medical school's affirmative action program was unconstitutional because under the "strict scrutiny" standard of review the university had not established that the separate admissions procedure was the least burdensome alternative available to attain the articulated goals of the program. Under a strict scrutiny standard, courts apply a heightened standard of review to determine the validity of governmental distinctions used, especially where the distinction is based on factors such as race or ethnicity. Concluding that the use of racial preferences was prohibited by the equal protection clause of the U.S. Constitution, the California court ordered Bakke's admission to the medical school. On review, the U.S. Supreme Court affirmed the California decision in part and reversed it in part, but failed to reach a clear consensus on the applicable law. Of the six opinions written in the case, none of which commanded a majority, three were noteworthy for the disparate conclusions they reached.

In the first opinion, written by Justice John Paul Stevens and joined by Justices Potter Stewart, William Rehnquist, and Chief Justice Warren Burger, the four justices declined to address the constitutional issues raised and relied instead on the general antidiscrimination provisions of Title VI of the Civil Rights Act to conclude that the Davis program's use of a quota for minority admissions had unlawfully discriminated against Bakke. They thereby upheld the part of the California decision ordering him to be admitted to the medical school. In the second opinion, Justice Lewis Powell concurred with the Stevens plurality in striking down the challenged quota system, although he did so on constitutional grounds. Thus a majority of five justices agreed that the medical school's admissions program was fatally flawed and should be struck down.

A different plurality of four justices, in the third opinion written by Justice William Brennan and joined by Justices Byron White, Thurgood Marshall, and Harry Blackmun, concluded that the use of a racial classification was permissible under both the Civil Rights Act and the U.S. Constitution as a means of overcoming the effects of past discrimination. These four justices were joined by Justice Powell in their view that some race-conscious university admissions programs were permissible, thereby reversing the part of the California court's decision that totally precluded the use of race in university admissions.

Justice Powell's separate opinion rejected the medical school's justifications for their affirmative action program, with one exception, namely, the school's interest in fostering the educational benefits that flowed from an ethnically diverse student body. "The attainment of a diverse student body . . .," he wrote, "clearly is a constitutionally permissible goal for an institution of higher education" (*Regents of the University of California* v. *Bakke,* 1978, p. 312). But echoing the earlier sentiments of Justice Douglas's dissent in the *DeFunis* case, Justice Powell declined to accept the adoption of racial quotas as a means of achieving such diversity in the classroom, stating that

> the nature of the state interest that would justify consideration of race or ethnic background . . . is not an interest in simple ethnic diversity, in which a specified percentage of the student body is in effect guaranteed to be members of select ethnic groups, with the remaining percentage an undifferentiated aggregation of students. The diversity that furthers a compelling state interest encompasses a far broader array of qualifications and characteristics of which racial or ethnic origin is but a single though important element. [Davis's] special admission program, focused *solely* on ethnic diversity, would hinder rather than further attainment of genuine diversity [p. 315].

Justice Powell turned to "the experience of other university admissions programs," which he believed demonstrated that race could be taken into account without reliance on a "fixed number of places to a minority group." His opinion quotes from a description of the Harvard University undergraduate admissions program, under which race or ethnic background could be deemed a plus factor in a particular applicant's file as long as it did not insulate the individual from comparison with all other candidates for the available seats. Justice Powell reasoned that the file of any particular minority applicant could be examined for his or her potential contribution to diversity without the factor of race being decisive when compared with that of a nonminority applicant "if the latter is thought to exhibit qualities more likely to promote beneficial educational pluralism." Justice Powell endorsed the consideration of qualities such as exceptional personal talents, unique work or service experience, leadership potential, maturity, demonstrated compassion, a history of overcoming disadvantage, ability to communicate with the poor, or other qualifications deemed important. He wrote, "In short, an admissions program operated in this way is flexible enough to consider all pertinent elements of diversity in light of the particular qualifications of each applicant, and to place them on the same footing for consideration, although not necessarily according them the same weight. . . . This kind of program treats each applicant as an individual in the admissions process" (pp. 317–318).

Furthermore, Justice Powell's opinion made it clear that remedying societal discrimination and increasing minorities in the profession were not valid state interests sufficient to justify any voluntary affirmative action program. Defining societal discrimination as "an amorphous concept of injury that may be ageless in its reach into the past," Powell wrote, "we have never approved a classification that aids persons perceived as members of relatively victimized groups at the expense of other innocent individuals in the absence of judicial, legislative, or administrative findings of constitutional or statutory violation" (p. 307). Finally, Powell remained unconvinced that the special admissions program was either needed or geared to promote the university's professed goal of improving the delivery of health care services to underserved minority communities.

By contrast, the Brennan plurality opinion expressly approved of preferential treatment for those who likely were disadvantaged by societal racial discrimination. Relying on past cases that interpreted Title VI of the Civil Rights Act, the Brennan opinion noted that such cases "compel the conclusion that States also may adopt race-conscious programs designed to overcome substantial, chronic minority underrepresentation where there is reason to believe that the evil addressed is a product of past racial discrimination" (p. 366). The Brennan opinion relied on prior cases to show that the state could adopt race-conscious programs if the purpose of such programs "is to remove the disparate racial impact its actions might otherwise have and if there is reason to believe that the disparate impact is itself the product of past discrimination, whether of its own or *that of society at large*" (p. 369; emphasis added).

Notwithstanding the divergence of opinions produced by the case, *Bakke* can be read for the conclusion that race or ethnicity could legitimately be factored into an admissions procedure, either to remedy past discrimination or to further a well-defined institutional goal of diversifying the student body, but only if the procedure entailed the same process of individualized comparison for all applicants without systematically excluding any group from consideration through the use of different application criteria or a different review body, and only where race or ethnicity was simply one factor under consideration.

In retrospect, the *Bakke* case was most significant because none of the Supreme Court justices absolutely foreclosed the use of race in an affirmative action program adopted in higher education. But while the *Bakke* decision upheld the remedial use of race or ethnicity in principle, it is also true that no clear consensus emerged from the various opinions regarding the scope of discriminatory behavior that could be redressed by the implementation of an institution's voluntary affirmative action programs. Thus, the important question of whether or not an educational institution had to have a history or record of prior discrimination before it could voluntarily implement a remedial program using race or ethnicity remained essentially unanswered by the Court.

Shortly after the decision, HEW issued a policy interpretation of Title VI in which the department reviewed its regulations under the act and concluded that no changes were required (44 Fed. Reg. 58509, Oct. 10, 1979). The policy interpretation included guidelines for applying the regulations consistent with the holding in *Bakke*. Thus, in cases in which the institution has engaged in prior discrimination on the basis of race, color, or national origin, the regulations required the institution to implement affirmative action programs to overcome the effects of that discrimination. Even in the absence of such discrimination, the regulations allow the institution to voluntarily adopt affirmative action programs where necessary to overcome the effects of conditions that result in limiting participation by persons of a particular race, color, or national origin (34 C.F.R. §§ 100.3ff).

Bakke was followed shortly by two state supreme court decisions that had significant impact on voluntary affirmative action programs in the states of Washington and California, and that relied heavily on the conclusions reached in both the Powell and Brennan opinions.

Post-*Bakke* Affirmation of the Use of Diversity

A year after *Bakke,* the Washington State Supreme Court, in *McDonald* v. *Hogness* (1979), upheld the University of Washington Medical School's admissions policy, under which race was considered in the category of "extenuating background circumstances" but was not listed explicitly as an admissions criterion. More significantly, under the university's affirmative action policy, minority applicants were not separately evaluated, nor did the policy provide for separate treatment or consideration of such applications.

The court held that McDonald would not have been admitted to the medical school even in the absence of any affirmative consideration of applicants' racial backgrounds, and it concluded that this showing alone was sufficient to deny the petitioner any relief. The court proceeded, however, to consider the discrimination claims on their merits because of their importance and because of the likelihood of their recurrence. In upholding the medical school's admissions program, the court relied heavily on Justice Powell's opinion permitting the use of race in admissions processes as long as there was no separate consideration of minority applications and only if minority applicants were not insulated from competition with remaining applicants. Comparing the University of Washington's program with the Harvard undergraduate admissions program referenced approvingly in Justice Powell's opinion, the court noted that because the University of Washington's program also operated "without a quota or separate consideration for minority groups but where race may be a beneficial factor," it possessed the "same redeeming characteristics" as the Harvard plan (*McDonald* v. *Hogness*, 1979, p. 713).

Noting that it had held, in its earlier *DeFunis* opinion, that eliminating racial imbalance within public legal education was a compelling state interest justifying the use of the university's affirmative action program, the *McDonald* court said that "in the instant case, the trial court determined the school had decided that, in order to serve the educational needs of the school and the medical needs of the region, the school should seek greater representation of minorities 'where there has been serious underrepresentation in the school and in the medical profession.' Thus, the program furthers a compelling purpose of eliminating racial imbalance within public medical education" (p. 714).

In the second post-*Bakke* case, *DeRonde* v. *Regents of the University of California* (1981), the plaintiff was an unsuccessful applicant to the University of California at Davis School of Law. Although he was subsequently admitted to and graduated from a different law school, the California State Supreme Court declined to dismiss the case as moot because of the need for resolution of "important issues of substantial and continuing public interest" (p. 222). The court noted that the law school admissions process relied principally on the applicant's predicted first-year average but other factors were also taken into consideration. In addition to growth, maturity, rigor of undergraduate studies, and commitment to study the law, the factors included economic disadvantage and ethnic minority status, which were seen as contributing factors to diversity.

The court noted that the primary reasons proffered by the law school for use of ethnic minority status were "first, an appreciable minority representation in the student body will contribute a valuable cultural diversity for both faculty and students; and second, a minority representation in the legal pool from which future professional and community leaders, public and private, are drawn will strengthen and preserve minority participation in the democratic process at all levels" (p. 223). The court was careful to emphasize that although minority status was included as one of several pertinent selection factors, the university did not employ any quota system or reserve a fixed number of positions for any minority applicants in its entering class.

Relying heavily on Justice Powell's *Bakke* opinion, the California court concluded that the Davis admissions procedure did not

> vary in any significant way from the Harvard program. Minority racial or ethnic origin was one of several competing factors used by the University to reach its ultimate decision whether or not to admit a particular applicant. Each application . . . was individually examined and evaluated in the light of the various positive and negative admissions factors. As Justice Powell pointedly observed, the primary and obvious defect in the quota system in *Bakke* was that it precluded individualized consideration of every applicant without regard to race. That fatal flaw does not appear in the admissions procedure before us. This is not a quota case [p. 225].

Turning to the acceptance of the Harvard admissions procedure in both the Powell and Brennan opinions in *Bakke,* the California court noted that such a plan was constitutional "so long as the use of race to achieve an integrated student body is necessitated by the lingering effects of past discrimination" (p. 225). The court concluded that the record amply established the existence of such prior discrimination, finding specifically that the evidence supported the use of a race-conscious admissions program to prevent a disproportionate underrepresentation of minorities at Davis, and noting that past societal discrimination against ethnic minorities was an unfortunate but demonstrable historical fact acknowledged in both the Powell and Brennan opinions. The *DeRonde* court further relied on the Brennan plurality's conclusion that the serious underrepresentation of minorities in medicine was the result of discrimination against minorities in education, in the medical profession, and in society in general. By clearly adopting both the diversity justification endorsed by Justice Powell and the necessity to mitigate the effects of historical discrimination as compelling state interests justifying remedial intervention, as broadly outlined in the Brennan opinion, the *McDonald* and *DeRonde* courts appeared to lend support to the vitality of voluntary affirmative action policies in use at the time.

In the decade that followed *Bakke* and its progeny, litigation over preferential admissions diminished as colleges and universities around the country modified their voluntary affirmative action policies to reflect the Supreme Court's judgment (O'Neil, 1987). Ongoing efforts by OCR to ensure institutional compliance with federal antidiscrimination regulations undoubtedly also contributed to the reduction in legal challenges brought on by so-called angry white males. In September 1992, for example, OCR entered into a voluntary conciliation and settlement agreement with the University at California at Berkeley, under which the law school agreed to end its practice of separating applicants into distinct pools, as well as its practice of employing separate waiting lists, based on race and ethnicity (OCR Case No. 10906001).

Recent Judicial Shifts: Narrowing the Standards

Recent federal cases that broach this issue appear to have reached contrary interpretations of the holding in *Bakke*. In *Davis v. Halpern* (1991), a federal district court reviewed the claim of an unsuccessful applicant to City University of New York Law School that the consideration of race in the school's admissions policy violated his constitutional and statutory rights. In ruling on the law school's motion for summary judgment, the court found that the plaintiff had established a prima facie case of discrimination with respect to race and ethnicity; the evidence clearly demonstrated that the law school had admitted minority applicants whose LSAT scores and grade point averages were lower than Davis's. Although the court recognized that the law school did not employ a racial quota in its admissions process, it remanded for jury consideration the issue of whether the law school's remedial measures were based on prior discrimination by the university itself or on the broader interests of remedying societal discrimination.

In concluding that the latter motivation was improper, the court noted that "the [Supreme] Court has also indicated that racial classifications whose purpose is remedial and justified by the need to correct and undo the damaging effects of a specific prior practice of discrimination could be upheld under the Equal Protection Clause. Such remedial measures cannot be justified by the existence of societal discrimination alone. Rather 'the Court has insisted on some showing of prior discrimination by the governmental unit involved before allowing limited use of racial classifications in order to remedy such discrimination' " (*Davis v. Halpern,*1991, p. 976, citing the U.S. Supreme Court opinion in *Wygant v. Jackson Bd. of Education,* 1986). This conclusion clearly conflicted with the reliance of the Brennan plurality in *Bakke* and the *DeRonde* court on the general need to counter societal discrimination as a factor justifying state deployment of race in the admissions process.

In a second federal case, *Hopwood v. Texas* (1996), the Fifth Circuit Court of Appeals concluded that certain minority group applicants (black and Mexican Americans) were treated differently by the University of Texas School of Law, which utilized a Texas Index (TI), a composite of the undergraduate grade point average and LSAT score, as a predictor of probable success in law school. Applicants fell into one of three "presumptive" TI groups, including "presumptive admit," "presumptive deny," and "discretionary zone." An applicant's TI level determined how extensive a review his or her application would receive. The court concluded that the law school not only maintained separate presumptive TI levels for the favored minority applicants but also employed a segregated application evaluation process under which black and Mexican American applications were reviewed by a minority subcommittee whose decisions were "virtually final," as well as maintained segregated waiting lists (pp. 935–937).

Although the court noted that Justice Powell had approved of the consideration of ethnicity as "one element in a range of factors a university properly may consider in attaining the goal of a heterogeneous student body" (*Regents of the University of California v. Bakke,*1978, p. 314), the Fifth Circuit court took issue with his conclusion that diversity was a sufficient justification for limited racial classification—a conclusion that was adopted in this case by the district court. The court stated in blunt terms that "Justice Powell's argument in *Bakke* garnered only his own vote and has never represented the view of a majority of the Court. . . . [His] view in *Bakke* is not binding precedent on this issue. While he announced the judgment, no other Justice joined in that part of the opinion discussing the diversity rationale. . . . Thus, only one Justice concluded that race could be used solely for the reason of obtaining a heterogeneous student body" (p. 944).

Relying on the U.S. Supreme Court's decisions in *Adarand Constructors v. Peña* (1995) and *City of Richmond v. J. A. Croson Co.* (1989), the court held that "recent Supreme Court precedent shows that the diversity interest will not satisfy strict scrutiny. Foremost, the Court appears to have decided that there is essentially only one compelling interest to justify racial classifications: remedying past wrongs" (p. 944). The court did not abandon absolute use of race, noting that "while the use of race per se is proscribed, state-supported schools may reasonably consider a host of factors—some of which may have some correlation with race—in making admissions decisions." The problem lay, the court held, with "the assumption . . . that a certain individual possesses characteristics by virtue of being a member of a certain racial group. . . . We do not opine on which way the law school should weigh Hopwood's qualifications; we only observe that 'diversity' can take many forms. To foster such diversity, state universities and law schools and other governmental entities must scrutinize applicants individually, rather than resorting to the dangerous proxy of race." The court concluded that "the use of race to achieve a diverse student body, whether as a proxy for permissible characteristics, simply cannot be a state interest compelling enough to meet the steep standard of strict scrutiny. These latter factors may, in fact, turn out to be substantially correlated with race, but the key is that race itself not be taken into account" (pp. 946–948).

Turning to the trial court's determination that the "remedial purpose of the law school's affirmative action program is a compelling government objective," the appellate court took issue with the trial court's reliance on the Texas school system as the government entity responsible for the discrimination being corrected. Relying on the U.S. Supreme Court's plurality opinion in *Wygant* (1986), the court noted, "The Supreme Court repeatedly warned that the use of racial remedies must be carefully limited, and a remedy reaching all education within a state addresses a putative injury that is vague and amorphous. It has 'no logical stopping point'" (p. 950). The court noted that the Texas legislature had not found that past segregation had present effects, that it had not determined the magnitude of such present effects, and that it had not carefully limited the plus that would be given to applicants to remedy that harm.

The appellate court also took issue with the district court's conclusion that, in evaluating whether the law school's affirmative action program served to overcome the present effects of past discrimination, the analysis of past discrimination should not be limited to the actions of the law school itself but could extend to the entire state educational system. The district court had found, for example, that Texas's long history of racially discriminatory practices in its primary and secondary schools in its not-too-distant past had three present effects at the University of Texas School of Law: "the law school's lingering reputation in the minority community, particularly with prospective students, as a 'white' school; an underrepresentation of minorities in the student body; and some perception that the law school is a hostile environment for minorities" (p. 939). Although the appellate court agreed that Texas had a history of racial discrimination, it declined to uphold the affirmative action program, either because the University of Texas system, rather than the law school, was the relevant past discriminator, or because the program was necessitated by the state's earlier agreement with OCR to bring the Texas public higher education system into compliance with Title VI.

Given its clear rejection of the Brennan plurality's use of societal discrimination and its restrictive interpretation of Justice Powell's diversity justification, *Hopwood* would appear to narrow considerably the allowable grounds for use of racial or ethnic factors in an admissions program. Although the *Hopwood* decision currently applies only to the Fifth Circuit, the impact of its holding may be far-reaching.

Race-Based Financial Aid

The *Hopwood* court also relied in part on the decision in *Podberesky* v. *Kirwan II* (1994) for its conclusion that "bad reputation" and "a hostile environment" were insufficient to sustain the use of race. In *Podberesky*, a Fourth Circuit case that struck down the use of race in awarding college scholarships, the appellant was a Hispanic male who challenged the University of Maryland at College Park's administration of several scholarship programs, including the Benjamin Banneker Program, that were restricted to students of African American heritage. The Banneker Program was intended as a partial remedy for past discriminatory action by the State of Maryland and was included in a package of recruitment plans and programs presented to OCR in 1979, following notification to the state ten years earlier that its higher education system was in clear violation of Title VI.

The appellate court had originally remanded the case because the district court had not specifically found that there were sufficient present effects of the university's past discrimination against African Americans to justify the maintenance of a race-restricted scholarship. Upon remand, the district court granted the university's motion for summary judgment because a strong evidentiary basis existed to support the existence of each of four present effects of past discrimination advanced by the university: that the university had a poor reputation within the African American community, that African Americans were underrepresented in the student population, that African American students who enrolled at the university had low retention and graduation rates, and that the atmosphere on campus was perceived as being hostile to African American students (p. 152).

Using the strict scrutiny standard of review, the court of appeals restated its two-step analysis requiring both a "strong basis in evidence for [the] conclusion that remedial action [is] necessary" and a showing that the remedial measure is "narrowly tailored to meet the remedial goal" (p. 153). The court rejected the first and fourth factors put forward by the university because "any poor reputation . . . is tied solely to the knowledge of the University's [past] discrimination" (p. 154). The court concluded that mere knowledge of historical fact was not the kind of present effect that could justify a race-exclusive remedy. With regard to the hostile climate claim, although the district court acknowledged that even northern universities had experienced de facto segregation in the past, the appellate court held that such societal discrimination was insufficient to satisfy the strict standard of review and to justify use of a race-based remedy.

In rejecting the other two factors, the appellate court took issue with the district court's resolution on a summary judgment motion of the issue of the correct reference pool to determine underrepresentation, holding that there were economic and other factors that may have contributed to the attrition rates of African Americans. The court also determined that the Banneker program was not narrowly tailored to remedy the underrepresentation and attrition problems, in part because of its purported attempts at recruitment of high-achieving African Americans, because the scholarships were open to non-Maryland residents, and because of the failure to correctly identify the reference pool against which the numbers of African American students who actually enrolled at UMCP were measured. Finally, the court held that the university had not made any attempt to show that it had tried without success any race-neutral solutions to the retention problem before adopting a race-exclusive scholarship program (pp. 158–160). Neither *Hopwood* nor *Podberesky* were subject to further review by the Supreme Court.

In 1991, while the *Podberesky* litigation was still pending, U.S. Secretary of Education Lamar Alexander issued a proposed Title VI Policy Guidance that would have required race neutrality in the awarding of college and university scholarships unless a court, administrative agency, or local legislative body identified present effects of past discrimination. After Secretary Alexander subsequently agreed to postpone the effective date of the policy guidance, several students sued the department in *Washington Legal Foundation* v. *Alexander* (1991), seeking a declaratory judgment that Title VI forbade colleges and universities that received federal funds from awarding race-exclusive scholarships, as well as an injunction requiring the department to issue regulations prohibiting all minority scholarships. The trial court dismissed all of the claims, holding that the plaintiffs had only a private cause of action against their college under Title VI, and the appellate court affirmed. Secretary Alexander was subsequently replaced by President Clinton's appointee, Richard Riley.

On February 23, 1994, the new education secretary issued final policy guidelines permitting colleges to continue to administer race-based financial aid or scholarship programs under certain conditions, including those in which "the aid is necessary to overcome the effects of past discrimination" or in order to further the goal of diversity (59 Fed. Reg. 8756). Colleges and universities not only could act pursuant to the order of a court, legislative body, or administrative agency, but could also determine on their own, without a prior determination by a judicial, administrative, or legislative body, that present effects of past discrimination existed on their campuses. In such cases, however, the college has to be prepared to demonstrate to a court or administrative agency that there is a strong basis in evidence for concluding that the college's action was necessary to remedy the effects of its past discrimination.

Thus, the awarding of university scholarships and financial aid to students on the basis of race and ethnicity follows limitations similar to administrative decisions governing college admissions. The guidelines require such use of race or national origin, along with consideration of other factors such as socioeconomic background or geographic origin, to be consistent with the constitutional standards reflected in Title VI, namely, that they be narrowly tailored to achieve the goal of a diverse student body, and only if such use does not unduly restrict access to financial aid for students who do not meet the race-based criteria. The guidelines outline several considerations that can be used for applying the narrowly tailored rule, including (59 Fed. Reg. 8756):

- Whether race-neutral means of achieving the goal of diversity have been or would be ineffective
- Whether a less extensive or intrusive use of race or national origin in awarding financial aid as a means of achieving that goal has been or would be ineffective
- Whether the use of race or national origin is of limited extent and duration and is applied in a flexible manner
- Whether the institution regularly examines its use of race or national origin in awarding financial aid to determine whether it is still necessary to achieve its goal
- Whether the effect of the use of race or national origin on students who are not beneficiaries of that use is sufficiently small and diffuse so as not to create an undue burden on their application to receive financial aid

The U.S. Supreme Court's ongoing failure to grant review in cases such as *Hopwood* and *Podberesky* increases the likelihood that the issues related to student affirmative action in higher education will not be resolved in the judicial arena any time soon. But that delay may not necessarily stifle the national debate in this contentious area, and proponents of affirmative action programs in higher education may soon find themselves engaged in the controversy at a new political level.

Statewide Referenda and the End of Racial Preferences

The day after the November 1996 elections in California, a lawsuit was filed in *Coalition for Economic Equity et al. v. Wilson* (1997), challenging the constitutionality of Proposition 209, the California Civil Rights Initiative, which passed by a 54 to 46 percent vote. The initiative proscribed discrimination against, or preferential treatment to, any individual or group on the basis of race, sex, color, ethnicity or national origin. Comparable initiatives have been proposed in the states of Florida and Washington, and the California proposition has even prompted a proposal for a federal civil rights act (Pavela, 1997).

In April 1997, the Ninth Circuit Court of Appeals reversed a district court ruling granting a preliminary injunction against the implementation of the proposition, broadly ruling that as a matter of law Proposition 209 did not violate the U.S. Constitution. The district court had provided extensive findings of fact and conclusion of law to support the issuance of the preliminary injunction. It concluded that the elimination of voluntary action to remedy past and present discrimination would reduce opportunities in public contracting and employment for women and minorities and would cause the enrollment of minority students in public institutions of higher education to fall. In its ruling the district court relied heavily on the U.S. Supreme Court cases of *Hunter v. Erickson* (1969) and *Washington v. Seattle School District No. 1* (1982) to conclude that the statewide proposition had a racial and gender focus that would impose a substantial political burden on the interests of women and minorities and was therefore unconstitutional.

In overruling the district court, the Ninth Circuit panel, noting that women and minorities in California constitute a majority of the state's electorate, asked rhetorically, "Is it possible for a majority of voters to impermissibly stack the political deck against itself" (p. 1441)? Concluding that it was not, and that Prop 209 was constitutional, the court stated:

> Plaintiffs challenge Proposition 209 not as an impediment to protection against unequal treatment but as an impediment to receiving preferential treatment. The controlling words, we must remember, are "equal" and "protection." Impediments to preferential treatment do not deny equal protection. . . . It is one thing to say that individuals have equal protection rights against political obstructions to equal treatment; it is quite another to say that individuals have equal protection rights against political obstructions to preferential treatment. While the Constitution protects against obstructions to equal treatment, it erects obstructions to preferential treatment by its own terms [p. 1445].

The Ninth Circuit declined to reconsider the matter *en banc* and the U.S. Supreme Court subsequently refused to consider the appeal.

Conclusion: Is *Bakke* Still Good Law?

To date, the *Bakke* case remains the first and only U.S. Supreme Court ruling regarding the validity of voluntary affirmative action programs in higher education. In light of the conflicting opinions rendered by the courts since that case was tried, it is useful to query what *Bakke* actually stands for and whether *Bakke* is still good law. Although the decision did not alter the Supreme Court's prior approval of the use of race in any context to compensate for past wrongs or omissions where there had been clear findings of prior discrimination, Justice Powell's reliance on a diversity rationale clearly was not shared by the Brennan plurality, which sought to rely more on notions of benign or ameliorative uses of race. Although technically Justice Powell's opinion was written for the majority, it is viewed by many as simply standing alone. More compelling is that since that time five of the current Supreme Court justices (Anthony Kennedy, Sandra Day O'Connor, William Rehnquist, Antonin Scalia, and Clarence Thomas) have cast some doubt on their commitment to diversity as an acceptable justification for affirmative action programs, albeit in cases arising in the employment context.

If *Bakke* still stands for any single precept, it must surely rest in Justice Powell's insistence that a race-based policy, if it is to pass constitutional muster, must include a process of individual comparisons that assures a measure of competition among all program applicants and does not result in the systematic exclusion of certain groups. Thus, race or ethnic background should become just one element in the selection process, and colleges and universities must carefully and narrowly tailor their processes to the specific circumstances facing their educational programs and to the particular student populations they seek to recruit and educate. Such judicial pronouncements—away from exclusively race-based remedies—tend to reflect the growing public sentiment in favor of a redefined sense of fairness in adopting redistributive measures. The creative college administrator should accordingly define the objects of an institution's quest for diversity along a broader spectrum to include individuals who have experienced educational disadvantage as a result of poverty, geographic location, physical disability, sexual orientation, and similar factors. Although some commentators (for example, Myers, 1997) believe that the growing institutional reliance on broad concepts of diversity as a substitute for race-based affirmative action undermines the historic and ongoing bases for such programs, the changing public attitudes and the evolving judicial temperament suggest that future efforts at remediation can occur only if such interventions improve the lot of the minority target group without consciously disadvantaging the majority.

Given the Supreme Court's failure to consider the case, the legal issues raised by Proposition 209 and similar proposed amendments in other states, as well as their profound implications for affirmative action programs in higher education, will undoubtedly continue to be debated for many years to come. Until the Supreme Court issues a definitive ruling in this area, college administrators can and should continue to focus specifically on the limited use of race in conducting individualized evaluations of applicants for admission and financial aid, and on drawing clear linkages to the role that racial and ethnic diversity plays in the fulfillment of their institutions' educational missions.

Court Cases Cited

Adams v. Richardson, 356 F.Supp. 92 (D.D.C. 1973), modified, 480 F.2d 1159 (1973) (en banc).

Adarand Constructors v. Peña, 115 S.Ct. 2097 (1995).

Bakke v. Regents of the University of California, 553 P.2d 1152 (Ca. 1976).

City of Richmond v. J. A. Croson Co., 488 U.S. 469 (1989).

Coalition for Economic Equity et al v. Wilson, 110 F.3d 1431 (9th Cir. 1997).

Davis v. Halpern, 768 F.Supp. 968 (E.D.N.Y. 1991).

DeFunis v. Odegaard, 507 P.2d 1169 (Wash. 1973), dismissed as moot, 416 U.S. 312 (1973), on remand, 529 P.2d 438 (Wash. 1974).

DeRonde v. Regents, 625 P.2d 220 (Ca. 1981).

Hopwood v. Texas, 78 F.3d 932 (5th Cir. 1996).

Hunter v. Erickson, 393 U.S. 385 (1969).

McDonald v. Hogness, 598 P.2d 707 (Wash. 1979).

Podberesky v. Kirwan I, 956 F.2d 52 (4th Cir. 1992).

Podberesky v. Kirwan II, 38 F.3d 147 (4th. Cir. 1994).

Regents of the University of California v. Bakke, 438 U.S. 265 (1978).

Washington v. Seattle School District No. 1, 458 U.S. 457 (1982).

Washington Legal Foundation v. Alexander, 778 F.Supp. 67 (D.D.C. 1991).

Wygant v. Jackson Bd. of Education, 476 U.S. 267 (1986).

References

Kaplin, W. A., and Lee, B. A. *The Law of Higher Education*. (3rd ed.) San Francisco: Jossey-Bass, 1995.

Myers, S. L. Jr. "Why Diversity Is a Smoke Screen for Affirmative Action." *Change,* July/Aug. 1997, pp. 25–32.

O'Neil, R. M. "Preferential Admissions Revisited: Some Reflections on *DeFunis* and *Bakke*." *Journal of College and University Law,* 1987, *14* (3) 423–434.

Pavela, G. *Synfax Weekly Report.* Jan. 13, 1997.

White, L. "Affirmative Action in Admissions and Financial Aid: An Introduction to Legal Analysis." Paper presented at the Stetson University Law and Higher Education Conference, Clearwater Beach, Fla., Feb. 12, 1996.

Alan T. Kolling is a law and policy analyst at the University of California, Berkeley, and a member of the State Bar of California.

Honest discussions about affirmative action will be impossible as long as those who challenge campus orthodoxy are vilified and silenced. A genuine commitment to diversity will include respect for ideological diversity and a realization that some critics of affirmative action may properly focus attention on the long-ignored issue of class and caste biases in American higher education.

What's Wrong with Race-Based Affirmative Action?

Gary Pavela

In 1996 a majority of Californians voted for Proposition 209, a measure prohibiting preferences based on race, sex, color, ethnicity, or national origin in public employment, education, and contracting. Many observers were surprised that a quarter of all minorities (nearly 40 percent of Asians) in one of the most diverse states in the nation voted in favor of the proposition. Likewise, 27 percent of California voters who defined themselves as liberals voted for 209, along with 31 percent of Democrats ("State Propositions. . .," 1996).

The complexity of the vote in California was not expressed in rhetoric about it. Some of the most outspoken opponents of Proposition 209 saw the outcome as a triumph of unmitigated racism. Speeches by Jesse Jackson, for example, reflected the view that California Governor Pete Wilson could be compared to George Wallace; that a vote for Proposition 209 was a vote for "ethnic cleansing" (Jackson, 1997, p. 3A); and that Ward Connerly (a black man who helped lead the campaign for the proposition) was a "house slave" (Bearak, 1997, p. 6).

The willingness of otherwise thoughtful and articulate figures like Jesse Jackson to demonize opponents of affirmative action may explain why college students are rarely willing to have open and candid discussions about issues related to race. It is well established, for example, that substantial numbers of college students have reservations about affirmative action, especially if it is seen as "preferences" ("New Students. . .," 1996, p. A33). Yet comparatively few students will discuss their opinions and concerns openly—a fact noted by Arthur Levine (1994, p. 185), who observed that "when we interviewed students on college campuses . . . we found it easier to talk with them about intimate details of their sex lives than . . . about race and gender differences."

Higher education may be engaging in a classic exercise of rigidly enforced "groupthink" when it comes to affirmative action. Aside from the obvious irony of enforcing ideological orthodoxy to protect diversity, educators may be cutting themselves off from good ideas and valid criticism—ideas and criticism that could help achieve the goals associated with affirmative action without destroying a broad consensus necessary for better race relations.

An example of the risks that higher education is running can be seen in another context: the adoption in 1996 of a new welfare bill deplored by many liberals. Upset by passage of the bill, New York Senator Daniel Patrick Moynihan observed, "For years, whenever the critics said, correctly, that the welfare system was doing more harm than good, and suggested it be rethought, its defenders screamed 'racism' and 'slavefare.' They did that until there was no public support left at all. Now they are stunned at what they are getting" (Apple, 1996, p. A16). Likewise, as long as opinion elites in higher education seek to marginalize even the most moderate critics of affirmative action, they set the stage for affirmative action's complete undoing.

Questioning Race-Based Preferences

Race-based affirmative action can be supported on the ground that blacks have had a unique "experience" in America, manifested in lingering racism that is hurtful even to the substantial numbers of blacks moving into the middle class and earning incomes higher than many whites. This argument has the potential to become its own undoing if taken too far.

Cornel West (1996) suggests that the essence of the experience of racism is to be viewed as "subhuman." That experience can be shared by a number of underrepresented groups—such as women in abusive relationships, openly gay people, poor people from Appalachia, and people with accents and cultural characteristics they cannot or will not change, such as some newly arrived immigrants or even an older generation of Americans from eastern and southern Europe whose names are suggestive of peasant ancestry or who are presumed to be connected with organized crime. The same experience can also occur on college campuses when whites males are said to have inherent (and unpleasant) white male characteristics—as if it made no difference, in the words of one observer, that one group of white males rode the freedom buses and another group burned them. All of these experiences are variations of being treated as less than human. It may prove intellectually dishonest and politically untenable in a democratic society to try to choose among the groups affected using some subjective scale to measure the degree of pain felt or insight gained.

Another problem with race-based group remedies in American society is that most Americans distrust such solutions, even if they are beneficiaries. As Seymour Martin Lipset argues in his book *American Exceptionalism* (1996), Americans have a long history of emphasizing equality of opportunity rather than equality of results. Accordingly, in Lipset's view, "white opposition to various forms of special governmental assistance for blacks and other minorities is in part a function of a general antagonism to statism and a preference for personal freedom in the American value system. . . ." (p. 141). This preference is of course not limited to whites. Lipset points out that it was also expressed by black abolitionist Frederick Douglass, who (in typical American fashion) "ridiculed the idea of racial quotas, as 'absurd as a matter of practice,' noting that it implied blacks 'should constitute one-eighth of the poets, statesmen, scholars, authors and philosophers' . . . and might promote 'an image of blacks as privileged wards of the state' " (p. 148).

The cultural current that Lipset describes is immensely strong. It formed a good part of the power of the "old" civil rights movement and helps explain that movement's success. Some academics may not like the American emphasis on individual freedom—and intellectual honesty requires an admission that it has been inconsistently applied. But the cultural emphasis on individualism does exist, has existed since the founding of the Republic, and is attracting new adherents daily (such as many of the latest immigrants seeking a "land of opportunity"). Any single institution—such as higher education—that directly challenges this emphasis will be blown away.

The Role of Class

In a September 1997 editorial questioning the rapid increase in college tuition rates, *The Washington Post* observed that "while university leaders continue to lay great, and proper, stress on their commitment to racial diversity—as, for example, in the tremendous hue and cry that has followed the California and Texas [moves] to limit affirmative action—you listen in vain for a comparably publicly expressed urgency on the need to keep the best of American higher education accessible to those (minority and otherwise) who can't dream of paying such [tuition] prices" ("Tuition Hike Ritual," 1997, p. C6). The *Post* has a point. While proponents of racial preferences deplore the shrinking enrollments of African Americans in Texas and California professional schools, and while opponents assert that minority enrollment will gradually be restored as more attention is paid to educating black and Hispanic elementary and secondary students, neither side is addressing the need for greater social and economic diversity at leading public and private universities across the country.

There has been one respected voice, however, calling for more social and economic diversity in higher education—a voice known for urging greater race and ethic diversity as well. Harold Hodgkinson, director of the Center for Democratic Policy, Institute for Educational Leadership, wrote in *Phi Delta Kappan* (1995) that "we have more effectively segregated people by wealth than we ever did by race." An exclusive focus on race alone, he believes, ignores the fact that "one-quarter of black households have higher incomes than the average white household." What is needed, in his view, is an understanding that "race [has] diverted our attention from the most urgent issue: *poverty reduces the quality of the lives of all children, regardless of race or ethnicity*" (pp. 176, 178; emphasis added).

Hodgkinson is an admired figure in higher education. His research about changing demographics in America is one reason that many colleges and universities moved faster than the corporate world to pursue racial diversity. The current attention he is paying to issues of class may presage a comparable shift on college campuses, especially as administrators look for alternatives to race-based affirmative action programs.

Considering Caste Rather than Race

A variation of class analysis that encompasses but is not limited by race is caste theory. Caste theory, as explained by Stanford history professor George M. Fredrickson (1996), "refers to a social arrangement rather than a fact of nature" (p. 16). It suggests that a wide variety of people (gays, many Appalachians, and most people of African ancestry) belong to groups with a history of subordination. Because numerous groups may be so identified, colleges will be driven to make personalized assessments of whether any particular individual might qualify for or benefit from a "plus" in college admissions. This approach is similar to what Supreme Court Justice William O. Douglas suggested in his dissenting opinion in *DeFunis* v. *Odegaard* (1973, pp. 331–332):

> [A] black [law school] applicant who pulled himself out of the ghetto into a junior college may thereby demonstrate a level of motivation, perseverance, and ability that would lead a fair-minded admissions committee to conclude that he shows more promise . . . than the son of a rich alumnus who achieved better grades at Harvard. . . . [A] poor Appalachian white . . . or some other American whose lineage is so diverse as to defy ethnic labels, may demonstrate similar potential. . . . Nor is there any bar to considering on an individual basis, rather than according to racial classifications, the likelihood that a particular candidate would more likely employ his legal skills to service communities that are not now adequately represented. . . .

Some assert that a caste approach to affirmative action can be used to disguise the reality of racism in American society. That is a risk, not an inevitability. It is also possible that educators might use caste theory to help people from many backgrounds understand the impact of racism. A good example is a speech by Mario Cuomo at a 1990 Italian-American Foundation dinner, reported by writer Mary McGory (1990, p. A2) in the *Washington Post*:

> He told tales they all could have told of ethnic slights and 'snide condescension.' He was first in his law school class at Fordham, but could not get a single interview on Wall Street. The dean suggested a name change. 'Can you imagine me with white shoes, bouncing up with a tennis racket saying. . . 'I went to Yale. I'm Mark Conrad.' They howled . . .[then he said] 'wouldn't it be a shame if we, having heard those cruel epithets of 'wop' and 'guinea' and 'dago,' were to sit back now and talk about the 'spics' and the 'niggers'? What

a shame it would be if those who were the victims of racism and stupidity should project it ourselves. . . .

The idea of caste is an affront to the reality and mythology of American individualism. Most Americans, however, can find some personal identification with a caste, now or in the past. This allows progressives to highlight the tension between theory and practice, and to draw on individualism as a progressive force, not an obstacle to social change. The heart of American progressivism is reflected in what Ralph Ellison wrote in a 1981 introduction to his *Invisible Man* (1995, p. xxii), where he observed that "revealing the human universals hidden within the plight of one who was both black and American" would challenge "strategies of division" based on "religion, class, color, and region." If that "strategy of division" could be defeated, Ellison believed, the result would be "a more or less natural recognition of the reality of black and white fraternity" (p. xxii).

Giving New Life—and an Honest Interpretation—to the *Bakke* Decision

Many traditional liberals appreciated Justice Louis Powell's nuanced opinion in *Regents of the University of California v. Bakke* (1978) which indicated that race could be but one element in a comprehensive admissions program designed to promote "genuine diversity" (as opposed to "simple ethnic diversity") on campus. They challenged the gradual expansion of race consciousness into overt racial set-asides, only to be labeled as racists by a new cohort of academic intellectuals, some associated with the critical race studies movement. Adherents to "critical race theory" (many of which are now signing newspaper advertisements for affirmative action that explicitly endorse Justice Powell's views in *Bakke*) knowingly ignored the limitations in Powell's opinion, thinking them hopelessly old-fashioned. Those thinkers designed new approaches, such as the segregated application evaluation procedure at the University of Texas School of Law. The latter sparked a challenge in *Hopwood v. Texas* (1996), resulting in a ruling precluding any consideration of race or ethnicity in the admissions process. Such are the fruits of insular self-righteousness and the absence of ideological diversity.

Higher education would be better off if a fraction of the energy spent evading the *Bakke* decision had been used to implement it. Still, some hope remains, reflected in the ongoing efforts of some legal scholars to provide an honest explanation of what *Bakke* means. The following exchange with Catholic University Law Professor William Kaplin appeared in *Synthesis: Law and Policy in Higher Education* (1997, p. 605):

SYNTHESIS: Assume a president at a public college outside the Fifth Circuit sought your advice on designing an affirmative action program likely to withstand a legal challenge. She reported that the university had no history of "official" segregation, but that enrollment of Hispanics and African-Americans was well below the proportion of potential students from those groups who would normally consider her institution. Her aim is to promote "diversity" on campus, by taking race into account in the admissions process. How can she do so with the best chance of legal success?

KAPLIN: The question here is whether "diversity" within a public college student body is a "compelling state interest" for purposes of equal protection analysis. In *Bakke,* Justice Powell said that it is, but he was writing for himself rather than a majority of the Court. Since *Bakke,* the Powell view has often been assumed to be the correct view, but the US Supreme Court has not ruled definitively on the issue. The 5th Circuit rejected the Powell view in *Hopwood*—the first US Court of Appeals to do so—but that decision is not binding on institutions in states outside the 5th circuit. Thus the current law is unclear and in flux, and it is unclear how the US Supreme Court would rule on the issue today. I believe I could muster enough legal support for the Powell view, however, that I could advise the president to proceed with a carefully crafted and well documented plan so long as the president understood there was a significant measure of risk.

SYNTHESIS: What is the Powell view on how the concept of "diversity" should be defined? How can administrators design an admissions standard that will meet his criteria?

KAPLIN: The "Powell" view is that achieving a diverse student body is a compelling interest that can justify the limited use of racial preferences in admissions. Powell would permit racial preferences when used in an admissions plan based on individualized evaluations of all applicants. All applicants must compete against one another for all the available slots. The race of the applicant can be considered as a "plus" that adds additional weight to a particular file but is nevertheless used in conjunction with rather than instead of other evaluative factors.

SYNTHESIS: Would you expect the Supreme Court to move beyond Powell's position and allow race to be the *exclusive* factor in promoting diversity?

KAPLIN: Although the Supreme Court may affirm the Powell position when an appropriate case comes before it, it is highly unlikely that the Court will move beyond the Powell position. Even to affirm the Powell position, the Court would have to affirm the Powell view that diversity is a compelling interest in the admissions context—a view that the *Hopwood* court rejected.

SYNTHESIS: What are we trying to accomplish when we speak of promoting "diversity" on campus? Is it a diversity of skin colors, experiences, ideas—or some combination of all three? What are the best legal arguments those who support race-conscious affirmative action can be making?

KAPLIN: Whatever "diversity" on campus is, it is not the same thing as diversity in the workplace or in government contracting programs or in other noneducational contexts. The best legal arguments, and the best policy arguments, for affirmative action programs promoting diversity must therefore focus specifically on the role diversity plays in fulfilling the mission of higher education institutions. In that regard, the most important aspect of diversity, in my view, would be diversity of life experience and the ways such diversity enriches academic discourse and campus community life within the institution. Racial diversity is not necessarily the only type of diversity to consider in this context.

Conclusion

Race-based affirmative action ignores the powerful reality of class and caste distinctions. It also runs against the strong strain of individualism in American life. The time has come for honest criticism and fresh thinking, grounded in Martin Luther King Jr.'s observation that "the Negro man must convince the white man that he seeks justice both for himself and the white man" (Valliant, 1977, p. 372). Until American colleges and universities return to that tradition—by honestly adhering to Justice Powell's opinion in the *Bakke* decision and by designing affirmative action programs that encompass both race and class—college and university administrators will never marshal the support necessary to achieve and maintain true diversity on campus.

Court Cases Cited

Regents of the University of California v. *Bakke,* 438 U.S. 265 (1978).
DeFunis v. *Odegaard,* 416 U.S. 312 (1973).
Hopwood v. *Texas,* 78 F. 3d 932 (5th Cir. 1996).

References

Apple, R. W. Jr. "His Battle Now Lost, Moynihan Still Cries Out." *New York Times,* Aug. 2, 1996, p. A16.

Bearak, B. "Questions of Race Run Deep for Foe of Preference." *New York Times,* July 27, 1997, p. 6 (electronic edition).

Ellison, R. "Introduction" to *Invisible Man.* New York: Vintage, 1995. ("Introduction" originally published 1981.)

Fredrickson, G. "Far from the Promised Land." *New York Review of Books,* Apr. 18, 1996, p. 16.

Hodgkinson, H. "What Shall We Call People." *Phi Delta Kappan,* Oct. 1995, pp. 176–178.

Jackson, J. "Jackson: King Would Be on Our Side." *USA TODAY,* Aug. 29, 1997 p. 3A.

Kaplin, W. "William Kaplin on Key Legal Issues in 1997." *Synthesis: Law and Policy in Higher Education.* Winter 1997, pp. 604–607.

Levine, A. "Paying Attention to Student Culture." *Synfax Weekly Report,* Jan. 31, 1994, p. 185.

Lipset, S. *American Exceptionalism.* New York: Norton, 1996.

McGory, M. "Cuomo's Ethnic Challenge." *Washington Post,* Oct. 23, 1990, p. A2.

"New Students Uncertain About Racial Preferences." *Chronicle of Higher Education,* Jan. 12, 1996, p. A33.

"State Propositions: A Snapshot of Voters." *Los Angeles Times,* Nov. 7, 1996, p. A29.

"Tuition Hike Ritual." *Washington Post,* Sept. 28, 1997, p. C6.

Valliant, G. *Adaptation to Life.* Boston: Little, Brown, 1977.

West, C. "Our Next Race Question." *Harper's Magazine,* Apr. 1996, p. 55.

GARY PAVELA is director of Judicial Programs at the University of Maryland, and editor of Synthesis: Law and Policy in Higher Education *and* Synfax Weekly Report, *from which portions of this chapter have been drawn.*

This chapter presents a review of the literature indicating the benefits of affirmative action and why it is necessary, as well as the results of a study to identify exemplary programs that are successful due to affirmative action.

Benefits of Affirmative Action in Student Affairs

Carol Logan Patitu, Melvin C. Terrell

Affirmative action efforts have been ongoing at colleges and universities for more than thirty years (American Council on Education, 1997). The goal has been to increase the number of people from underrepresented groups in higher education and to diversify colleges and universities. This goal is beginning to be realized as numbers have increased with the support of affirmative action programs; however, there remains room for improvement of minority representation in higher education. With affirmative action under attack it is crucial to be aware of what affirmative action has helped to achieve for minorities in higher education. The research discussed in this chapter reveals the major gains that minorities have made, and it highlights student affairs programs, services, and activities that have been successful due to affirmative action. The purpose of the chapter is to promote awareness of the many benefits that minorities, and indeed everyone in higher education, have experienced due to affirmative action.

Before Affirmative Action

Before affirmative action became an issue, institutions in the United States were ostensibly merit-based systems, but unfortunately they often operated poorly (López, Colson, and Schaberg, 1996). Until relatively recently, most educational systems did not seriously consider either women or minorities for most positions. Systems often relied on "connections" more than anything else, and universities admitted students from the same limited clusters of schools and families (López, Colson, and Schaberg, 1996). The standards used were unjust not only to women and minorities but to everyone who would benefit from diversity and from exposure to different cultures.

In pre-affirmative-action times, colleges and universities relied heavily on assessment test scores (such as ACT and SAT) and transcripts to judge merit and predict success. Merit can be described as the ability to contribute to valid institutional goals. To base admittance and hiring purely on merit means to award positions to candidates who are most qualified to perform successfully. Measures of merit utilized for admission to colleges and universities and for hiring of faculty and administration are imperfect. "No test or set of tests is a completely accurate or unbiased predictor, and the better tests may be too expensive to use. Moreover, the process of selecting students, [and] employees . . . is rarely an analytically precise choice based on reliably measured attributes" (López, Colson, and Schaberg, 1996, section 3.111).

As López and colleagues (1996) assert, nothing is written in stone describing what constitutes a competent performance and what predictors qualify a candidate to do a specific task well. Instead, university personnel base their decisions on their experiences and on devise predictors. Almost everyone acknowledged, even before affirmative action, that standardized exams were supposed to bypass the prejudices and abuse of individual discretion "and, hopefully, [become] a positive step in the evolution of justifiable selection criteria" (López, Colson, and Schaberg 1996, section 3.111).

Affirmative Action in Student Affairs

As Shackelford and Shackelford (1995) indicate, affirmative action began as "a well-intentioned effort to remedy the effects of discrimination" (p. 25). Affirmative action counteracts discrimination and attempts to ensure equitable and merit-based treatment of all individuals applying for college or for the workplace (Shackelford and Shackelford, 1995; Hispanic Association of Colleges and Universities, 1995).

Few deny the progress that has been made since affirmative action began. Yet those who do claim that affirmative action cannot confidently take credit for that progress. Of course, it would be a stretch for anyone to make this sort of claim about anything, affirmative action included. Progress has been caused by many complex factors, making it difficult to isolate a principle or major cause. Others insist that we no longer need affirmative action even though it has played a role in fighting discrimination and in opening up opportunities. It is these claims that the literature addresses. "Meanwhile, at least in the minds of the great majority of those who make the decisions about filling merit-based slots, affirmative action has played a central role in the change we've seen" (López, Colson, and Schaberg, 1996, section 3.22). Through both the triumphs and the defeats, valuable experience has been acquired.

For the past thirty years, affirmative action has worked for higher education in several ways to affect admissions policies and procedures, the hiring of faculty and staff, the distribution of funding for men's and women's athletic teams, minority scholarships, training for teachers who serve minority populations, and government funding (Hispanic Association of Colleges and Universities, 1995). The definition of underrepresented groups has been expanded to include not only racial and ethnic minorities but also women, the disabled, and other groups (Shackelford and Shackelford, 1995). Altman and Promís (1994) define affirmative action as "actively seeking to hire or promote women and persons whose ethnic heritage is Hispanic, African, Asian or Native American" (pp. 11–12). Programs related to affirmative action include multicultural centers and minority internships, which are designed to improve access and retention for minorities. Specific affirmative action programs include the Federal Early Outreach and Student Services Programs known collectively as TRIO; Minority Science Improvement; Women's Educational Equity; Indian Education; Early Intervention Scholarships, Partnerships, and Summer Programs; Minority Teacher Recruitment and Training Services; Bilingual Education and Faculty Development Fellowships; Minority/Multicultural Centers; and Minority Mentoring Fellowships (Hispanic Association of Colleges and Universities, 1995). Many of these programs involve the university's student affairs department. As Jones, Terrell, and Duggar (1991) assert, "The role of chief student personnel officers may be pivotal in the willingness to view objectively the role of cultural diversity, to interpret cultural diversity in the context of institutional missions, and to encourage the allocation of resources (human and capital) on campuses" (p. 126).

Many examples of student affairs affirmative action initiatives can be found in the literature. For example, Wagner (1992) describes several initiatives that take place at the University of California–Berkeley, which attracts minority students on the bases of its faculty reputation, geographical location, and aggressive leadership by the dean's office. To increase minority student enrollment, the university provided funds for potential students to visit campuses and conferences, put energy and research into recruitment, and visited more than thirty campuses within and outside the state. Berkeley also established a first-year graduate mentorship program, graduate research assistantship and mentorship program, and a dissertation-year fellowship program (Wagner, 1992).

According to Gomez (1997), "the racial and ethnic makeup of the Berkeley undergraduate student body has changed tremendously as a result of affirmative action programs" (p. 3). In 1968, only about 2.8 percent of students attending Berkeley were African Americans and 1.3 percent were Latino, despite the large African American and Latino population of California. In 1994, the numbers rose, with 38 percent of the entering class Asian American, 34 percent white, 14 percent Latino, and 6 percent African American. Through its efforts, the university has increased minority participation in the graduate school, with 25 percent of English doctoral students identified as African American or Hispanic. In biological sciences studies, minority enrollment has also increased (Wagner, 1992).

According to Wagner, an example of a national program is found in the Dorothy Danforth Compton (DDC) Minority Fellowship Program, started in 1981 to aid minority students preparing for careers in college or university teaching. Ten universities throughout the United States participate and receive funding for their recruitment and retention activities (Wagner, 1992). Participating universities have included Brown University, the University of California at Los Angeles, the University of Chicago, Columbia University, Howard University, Stanford University, the University of Texas at Austin, Vanderbilt University, the University of Washington, and Yale University. Fellows receive graduate stipends and environmental support through the program and participate in a national conference held every other year, during which minority faculty share their experiences and give support. By 1992, seventy DDC fellows had attained their doctorates (Wagner, 1992).

College Participation and Enrollment

College participation is the area to which many researchers have turned when assessing the success of affirmative action. They have found that underrepresented groups have experienced enrollment gains, have increased undergraduate and graduate degree attainment, and have made gains in higher education employment. These rates differ, however, by race, gender, and ethnicity. Though African Americans and Hispanic Americans were the minority groups to experience the greatest increase in numbers in higher education during the late 1980s and early 1990s, their numbers continue to be much lower than those of whites attending college (American Council on Education, 1997).

According to the American Council on Education's (1997) report on affirmative action, which studied enrollment in several universities throughout the United States for its *1995–96 Status Report on Minorities in Higher Education,* minority college enrollment increased by 63 percent from 1983 to 1993. Minority undergraduate enrollment rose by 62 percent, while graduate and professional school enrollment increased by 82 percent and 107 percent respectively. Gains differed by race and ethnicity, however. "With close to a doubling in their total enrollment, Asian Americans and Hispanic Americans experienced the largest increases, compared with gains of 52 percent for American Indians and 35 percent for African Americans." Fifty-five percent of all college students were women in 1994.

In terms of college degrees earned, minorities showed tremendous progress. According to *Black Issues in Higher Education* (Borden, 1996), the total number of degrees conferred annually from 1988 through 1993 increased from 1.9 million to 2.2 million, a difference of 17 percent, with the annual percentage increase in degrees earned by minorities and non–U.S. citizens more than double the rate of degrees earned by whites. According to the American Council on Education (1997), between 1985 and 1993 bachelor's degrees awarded to African Americans increased by 36 percent; to American Indians, by 34 percent; to Hispanic Americans, by 75 percent; and to Asian Americans, by nearly 103 percent. The National Collegiate Athletic Association's college completion data for 1990–1994 also indicates increases in the rate of graduations for minority athletes. There was only a 3 percent higher graduation rate for Asian Americans, however, and an 8 percent increase for American Indians (American Council on Education, 1997). African Americans and Hispanic Americans also showed more gains in graduation rates than whites, gaining 7 and 5 percent respectively, compared to a gain of only 3 percent for whites. "Despite these gains, African-Americans, American Indians, and Hispanics continue to trail whites in overall graduation rates" (American Council on Education, 1997, para. 13).

What If There Was No Affirmative Action?

Some of those who argue against affirmative action claim that the gains in college participation and enrollment are due to many factors, which may or may not include affirmative action. This claim inspires the question in the minds of affirmative action's supporters, Where would minority students stand today if there had been no affirmative action in our colleges and universities? This is a compelling question that has no absolute answer. The literature does not attempt to answer it, except perhaps to say that the number of minority students enrolled in and completing higher education would not have increased as they did.

Cross (1994a) assessed the impact of affirmative action specifically on African American admissions. Since affirmative action began, about fifteen thousand African Americans have graduated from the Ivy League colleges and universities. According to Cross, "Few people will dispute the fact that under standard, though highly controversial, measures of academic ability, college-bound African-American students as a group are far less prepared in academic terms to compete for admission into American colleges and universities than are their white counterparts" (1994a, p. 45). Cross examined how affirmative action probably affected the numbers of African American students admitted to our nation's top colleges and universities by looking specifically at academic preparation as measured by SAT scores. Whether or not SAT scores are a proper measure of the academic qualifications of all students, they are currently a major part of the acceptance process at such institutions.

For example, Cross was able to correlate admissions with SAT scores at Harvard University. The mean SAT score of African American freshmen entering Harvard University was 160 points below the average score of admitted whites. African Americans averaged combined scores of 1290 and whites averaged combined scores of 1450. For Harvard in particular, affirmative action was responsible for a large portion of the African American freshmen being admitted. Through similar calculations, Cross determined that "under strict merit-based admissions based solely on SAT scores," African-Americans would make up only about 1.5 percent of admissions to the nation's top colleges and universities. "Instead of 3,000 African American freshmen at the nation's 25 top-rated schools, we would have less than 700" (1994b, p. 53). Cross has clearly provided evidence that affirmative action has benefited African Americans in higher education.

Next ppr.

Students Benefit from Diversity and Multiculturalism

There are many ways that students benefit from diversity, including being prepared to be members of a global community, having their intercultural communication skills enhanced, becoming aware of and more sensitive to cultural differences, being exposed to views unlike their own, and being allowed to confront and discuss multicultural issues. Additionally, diversity prepares students for an "international, multicultural, increasingly interdependent world" (Scott, 1992, p. 2). To make use of current travel and communications capabilities, students will need skills in and awareness of language and culture (Scott, 1992).

It is important to expose students to views besides those of the majority and their own, both in and out of the classroom. The diverse academy "provides the opportunity to constantly examine and debate competing propositions to create a dialogue that will help us reach a better understanding of the truth" (Chahin, 1993, p. 4). A successful forum in the university depends on "intellectual diversity that includes other kinds of diversities—cultural, racial, gender, sexual, social, and economic" (p. 5).

Astin (1993b) found empirical support for the effects of diversity through his national four-year longitudinal study of student outcomes. He distributed surveys to 25,000 undergraduates at 217 four-year colleges and universities. On the basis of this study Astin (1993a) concludes that "emphasizing diversity either as a matter of institutional policy or in faculty research and teaching, as well as providing students with curricular and extra-curricular opportunities to confront racial and multicultural issues, are all associated with widespread beneficial effects on a student's cognitive and affective development" (p. 45). The effects of institutional diversity emphasis include heightened cultural awareness and satisfaction. Student diversity experiences—in which students socialized with persons from different racial and ethnic groups—were found to have a strong positive effect on cultural awareness, commitment to promoting racial understanding, and academic development and satisfaction with college (Astin, 1993a). African-American author Manning Marable summed it up well when he said, "Educational excellence, especially in our internationalized world, is best achieved when people interact with others from different faiths, nationalities, from divergent cultures and racial identities. Diversity is at the heart of academic excellence" (cited in Rockwell, 1997, para. 12).

Successful Programs

The literature strongly suggests that affirmative action is a beneficial program when it is carried out by executive leadership. To determine specifically whether affirmative action translates into positive gains for minority students in the area of student affairs, a research project was undertaken by the authors of this chapter. It was designed to identify and highlight exemplary programs.

A random sample of student affairs practitioners was selected, including the presidents of seven national organizations and twenty-three commission chairs of one of these organizations. Additionally, nine other institutions participated that were recommended by the presidents or commission chairs of the other organizations, providing a total of thirty-nine participants. Subjects completed a survey called Successful Student Affairs Programs Due to Affirmative Action. On the survey, participants were asked to name student affairs programs, services, or activities in their organization or institution that had been successful due to affirmative action. They were then asked to describe these successful programs and state why they have been successful, and to provide additional comments and the name and location of other successful programs. Subjects were sent a letter of explanation, a stamped return envelope, and a copy of the survey instrument. Additionally, participants were told that the findings would be shared with them. A follow-up mailing was completed to obtain a higher response rate. To the thirty-nine surveys mailed there were nineteen responses, a response rate of 49 percent.

Minority and Multicultural Programs and Centers. Holyoke Community College's Students Together Reach Individual Vision of Excellence (STRIVE) Program is a federally funded TRIO program that reaches out to two hundred nontraditional high potential and transfer-oriented students who are the first generation to go to college, disabled, and low income and assists them in completing a two-year degree and making the transition to four-year colleges and universities. The graduation rate for minority students at Holyoke Community College has increased significantly since the inception of the program in 1987.

University of Maryland programs include the funding of various cultural celebrations; celebration months have taken place each year for the past ten years. Desegregation funding ($6,000 to $10,000 annually) and staff resources have been used to plan, market, and produce programs, and to advise committees for Asian, Latino, African American, gay and lesbian, and women's weeks, months, or both. In addition, a significant award has been given to an outstanding African American student leader annually for the past twelve years, and a scholarship has been provided for underrepresented populations. Student leadership conferences or summits for specific ethnic and cultural groups have been hosted annually for the past eight years, and funding has been provided for national and regional conference attendance. Additionally, the African American Culture Center, which cost $1.5 million, was constructed. Research was conducted with students and admissions candidates to ascertain the experiences of different populations. Western Michigan University's Office of Student Life advises many multicultural student organizations, including the Minority Student Organization, and sometimes helps with their events.

Rio Salado Community College (RSCC), in Tempe, Arizona, a Maricopa Community College, hosts the Literacy and High School Diploma Equivalency Programs that are provided throughout Maricopa County. RSCC also provides

Reach Out, a program funded by the A.P. Sloan Foundation that uses the concept of asynchronous programming with GED and other at-risk students to provide distance modality courses to students who might not otherwise be able to attend college. The most recent partnerships include provision of distance learning to the Fort McDowell Indian Community. The Public Broadcasting Station featured the success of the Reach Out program in a documentary on distance learning aired in spring 1998.

The Native American Education Office of Glendale Community College, Glendale, Arizona, provides support services to Native American students, and other services, including outreach to reservation communities. Native Americans enrolled in the high school to community college bridge program have a 96.6 percent success rate that is attributed to the support services offered by the program. The American Indian/Multicultural Center at Mesa Community College is the most extensive program in Maricopa Community Colleges to serve Native American students. It was formed in 1986–87 as an affirmative action committee and evolved into an affirmative action advisory board that meets on a monthly basis. An Indian services center was formed and grew into a multicultural center with a diverse staff. The center is involved in several areas, including personnel (ensuring that two out of five search committee members are members of minority groups), outreach (conducting on-site visitations at nineteen reservations), a college orientation program, diversity training, transfer services, and research on the success of new hires and on gender and ethnicity issues.

Hiring Practices. In the financial aid office of the University of Montana, a minority employee was hired specifically to help minority students with financial aid. The position allowed the financial aid office to target extra help to minority students, especially American Indian students. The number of students receiving aid has increased significantly (more than 25 percent), which is part of the reason it was started. Another program enriched with special fellowship and hiring programs for minorities was the University of Maryland's graduate assistant program.

Special Populations. At the University of Texas at El Paso, the Tutoring and Learning Center implemented a state-of-the art technology room to meet the special needs of disabled students with the help of Disabled Student Services and the Equal Opportunity Commission office. The University of Texas at El Paso's Disabled Student Services trains tutors and instructors to work with diverse populations, including those with physical disabilities and learning-disabled students. A conference on fostering diversity in leadership in student affairs was jointly sponsored by the Tutoring and Learning Center, the American College Personnel Association, the Texas Association of College and University Personnel Administrators, the Division of Student Affairs, and the El Paso Community College. Ongoing cooperative staff development between El Paso Community College and the city of El Paso is the expected outcome.

Disabled Student Resources and Services assists students with disabilities at Western Michigan University (WMU), Kalamzoo, to seek effective accommodations, develop their abilities, and increase their independence. It provides advocacy and referral within the WMU and Kalamazoo communities, writes advocacy letters to professors, assists in early registration, and provides a library of taped textbooks and assistance with securing taped texts, volunteer readers, campus transportation, and adaptive computer equipment. The university's adaptive technology laboratory provides speech synthesis and screen enlargement, refreshable Braille display, and voice input technology.

Another successful program is the Holyoke Community College Office for Students with Disabilities. This program provides outreach and academic accommodations for three hundred disabled students each year. Its student advisory board provides advocacy for students and works with the community to help high school students and their parents understand the transition to college. Significant numbers of these students take college leadership positions and transfer to four-year institutions. Their graduation rate has increased by 60 percent since the program started in 1988.

WMU's Women's Resources and Services, a division of the Office of Student Life, successfully provides educational programs and materials and personal assistance to students, focusing on issues that are of special interest not only to women but also to an increasing number of men, particularly sexual assault, sexual harassment, and abuse and violence in relationships. The program hosts educational programs and victim assistance services, and it disseminates information and resources.

WMU's Office for Lesbian, Bisexual and Gay issues (also part of the Office of Student Life) promotes an environment that is affirmative and supportive of sexual orientation to provide support to any individual on campus who is struggling with such issues and to help educate the WMU community about issues related to the diversity in sexual orientation on the campus. This program includes educational programs, support and advocacy for human and civil rights, and networking with other organizations who are addressing the concerns of lesbian, bisexual, and gay individuals.

Religious Affiliations and Campus Ministries. The Office of Student Life at WMU fosters enrichment and belonging in the campus community through several services, including the Office of Religious Activities. WMU's Kanely Memorial Chapel is designed to serve as a center for worship-oriented and action-oriented religious concerns. In addition to the Chapel Office, several campus ministers maintain offices in the building. Many student religious organizations, WMU departments, and the community use the facilities for their gatherings. The university provides a brochure listing the diverse religious groups that meet on campus, including Ancient Altars (a shamanistic nature religion), the Buddhadharma Society, the Campus Bible Fellowship, and the Hillel Foundation.

Community Outreach. The Mentor Program at Holyoke Community College reaches out to Latina pregnant and parenting teens and high school dropouts in the local community who are trying to finish their high school education or obtain a GED. Bilingual student mentors serve as role models and provide support, referrals, tutoring, campus tours, and other services. Now in its fourth year, the Mentor Program has assisted more than six hundred high school dropouts, at least half of whom have earned their GED and sixty of whom have gone on to enter community colleges. The English as a Second Language (ESL) Support Program, an outreach and support program at Holyoke Community College, has been in action for twelve years. During that time, enrollment of Hispanic students at the college has increased by 400 percent. Hispanic students are now graduating in record numbers. Other services for students include ESL instruction, counseling, tutoring, and other supportive activities.

The bilingual staff and tutors of the Multicultural Affairs Program at Glendale Community College, Glendale, Arizona, collaborate closely with the community to respond effectively to student and community needs. Formed in 1975–76, the program actively pursues postsecondary educational opportunities for minority youth and underrepresented adults. It serves high school minority graduates, high school dropouts, and community adults in career change or enhancement and in retraining or learning special skills, and it works with enrolled students who need assistance or information to facilitate the pursuit of their educational goals. The program interacts with at-risk programs and referral structures and systems and community organizations, and it performs early outreach for schools and communities. In addition, the program facilitates admissions, financial aid, educational planning, and follow-up. The director of the Multicultural Affairs Program believes that his department will remain a vibrant part of the college structure because it is more than cost-effective. Glendale College leads the transfer of Maricopa Community College's minority students to four-year institutions. The director has published a number of articles, available through ERIC, on the retention and success of multicultural students.

Success in these programs is attributed to recognition of obstacles to minority participation in higher education; networks with key education and community leaders and officials who have visible sentiments toward disadvantaged students and minorities and their educational attainment; and an established strong presence in the service area as well as credibility in being able to successfully serve and guide economically and educationally disadvantaged youth and community adults. The community is 81.9 percent white, 1.7 percent Native American, 2.7 percent African American, 11.8 percent Hispanic, and 1.9 percent Asian. The participation rate in the service area for Fall 1996 was 17,647 total participants made up of the following groups: 73.1 percent (12,897) white, 1.4 percent (252) Native American, 3.9 percent (694) African American, 14.0 percent (2,470) Hispanic, and 3.8 percent (671) Asian. In Spring 1997, 72.1 percent (11,769) were white, 1.5 percent (241) were Native American, 4.3 percent (695) were African American, 14.5 percent (2,439) were Hispanic, and 4.1 percent were (665) Asian.

Assessment of average credits attempted versus credits earned provides an indicator of persistence. There was a significantly higher persistence rate than at national community and two-year colleges (as reported by the Western Interstate Commission on Higher Education and the American Association of Community Colleges), for the fall semester. The average for all student groups was in the range of 83 percent for white students, 85 percent for Asian students, 79 percent for Hispanic students, 76 percent for African American students, and 74 percent for Native American students. Major initiatives include participation in the YMCA Minority Achievement Program and Saturday Academies for minority students, and continuation of the Drysart Bilingual Program in adult education at El Mirage School. Project Intervention, a partnership with Glendale Community Housing Development Organization, Glendale Elementary School District, and Glendale Community College, was developed and successfully implemented to address the educational and training needs of disadvantaged central Glendale residents.

Adult Reentry Program. Holyoke Community College's New Directions, New Careers program is a reentry program for 150 adult students who are primarily single parents, academically underprepared, and low income. The program provides advocacy for women on Aid to Families with Dependent Children and encourages students to explore nontraditional careers. Services include an intensive first semester of academic support, and learning communities designed to foster cohesion and social comfort on the campus. The students in the program have the highest retention and graduation rate of all students at the college.

Recruitment. Mesa Community College is involved in Native American Partnerships with 602 students enrolled in the Native American Recruitment Program. The program visits sixteen high schools located in Indian reservation communities. The program provides on-site advisement, testing, career planning, academic registration, orientations, financial aid and scholarship searches, counseling, bridge programs, and student life support systems. More than four hundred Native Americans are recruited each year to attend Mesa Community College or other Maricopa Community Colleges. The Native American Education Center provides career orientations and academic support services to Native American high school dropouts from the unified school district.

The Mathematics, Engineering, and Science Achievement (MESA) program at the University of Arizona was designed to increase the number of historically underrepresented ethnic groups in professions related to mathematics, engineering, and the physical sciences by developing strong academic and leadership skills, raising educational and career expectations, and building a positive self-image among Arizona's Hispanic, African American, and Native American students. Statewide, MESA operates in fourteen school districts and is active in nine middle schools and seventeen high schools. Locally, MESA operates in four school districts, is active in six middle schools and nine high schools, and has more than five hundred students enrolled in the program. Services include tutoring in mathematics, science, and English; awarding tuition fee waivers to select qualified, outstanding MESA students who attend the University of Arizona; and making Incentive Awards for maintaining or achieving high grades in math-based fields and English. The MESA program sponsors a variety of activities, including guest speakers, Saturday Academies, SAT/PSAT workshops, engineering activities, field trips, design projects, and academic competitions. Students who have participated in the MESA program have a greater chance of enrolling in the fields of math, science, or engineering. The University of Arizona's overall minority enrollment in these areas is 25 percent, while MESA students' enrollment in these fields is 50 percent.

Academic Preparation for Excellence (APEX) at the University of Arizona was established in 1984. The program serves eleven school districts in Southern Arizona with site-based programming beginning in the sixth grade. The mission of the program is to increase the number of ethnic minority, economically disadvantaged, or first-generation college-bound students who successfully enter higher education. APEX provides tutoring in math, science, and English; workshops; tuition fee waivers; book scholarships to qualified, outstanding APEX students who elect to attend the University of Arizona; and campus visits. A component of the APEX programs matches APEX students with mentors who are either community professionals or University of Arizona students. The mentors demonstrate the value of education, share their knowledge and experience, and become a friend and role model. In the last four years, 90 percent of students involved in the APEX program enrolled in college, and their persistence rates are higher than those not in the program. During the past ten years, the University of Arizona moved from 7 percent to 19 percent minority representation. APEX operates in ten Southern Arizona school districts, in forty-one middle schools and high schools, and has more than two thousand students enrolled in the program.

Professional Organizations

The American College Personnel Association (ACPA) has created standing committees for representation of constituency-based groups on its executive council, and affirmative action officers to monitor affirmative action goals of the association, aiming to increase membership of persons of color from the current 15 percent to 21 percent; of gay, lesbian, and bisexual persons, to 10 percent, and persons with disabilities to 10 percent. A postcard survey returned directly to the affirmative action officer was included in all new and renewing member packets. The ACPA has also made efforts to establish a modest funding pool to support initiatives that further the affirmative action goals of the association.

In 1996, the budget allocated $10,000 to support initiatives to advance the association's affirmative action goals. All but one of the nine projects received full or partial funding. These projects included the South Dakota College Personnel Association, support for Native American college personnel professionals to attend the state conference and to join the ACPA, and the Commission I Task force on disability, which assesses the national convention with regard to issues of accessibility in order to enhance membership of professionals with disabilities. A report is in progress and the assessment of the association's services is ongoing.

In 1997, with a funding base of $9,000, ten projects were funded. Initiatives included the task force on disabilities, which assessed the degree to which the 1996 annual convention provided a welcoming environment for people with disabilities and began assessment of ACPA member services, and a "Signed Supper" program at the 1997 Chicago convention, which brought together deaf attendees and others interested in this population. The report was prepared and submitted to planning teams. Regarding the ACPA affirmative action initiatives, Joanne Risacher wrote, "I believe this initiative is one that any organization could duplicate easily and with a relatively small amount of set-aside funds" (personal communication, July 17, 1997).

The National Association of Student Personnel Administrators (NASPA) has several diversity initiatives, including the Minority Undergraduate Fellows Program (MUFP), which has been very successful. The purpose of the program is to identify and cultivate talented ethnic minority students (African, Asian, Hispanic, or Native American) who are completing the sophomore year or the second year in a two-year transfer program and who demonstrate academic promise. The MUFP fosters the students' personal and professional development, provides support and encouragement to students as they complete their degree requirements, and promotes enrollment in masters-and doctoral-level programs for careers in student affairs and higher education.

The MUFP was initiated in 1989 to provide participants with knowledge, insight, and understanding of the opportunities available in student affairs and higher education; opportunities to engage in mentoring and networking experiences; and experiences in student affairs and higher education. To meet these goals, the program offers three components: participation in a one-or two-year campus-based internship or field work experience under the guidance of a mentor; participation in a Summer Leadership Institute, an intensive three-day program of lectures, workshops, and panel discussions; and participation in an eight-week paid summer internship in higher education for serious, career-minded second-year fellows (NASPA, 1996).

Of the MUFP fellows in the class of 1996, 85.7 percent (eighteen of twenty-one fellows) believed they had been successful in meeting the goals they had set; 57.1 percent rated the overall experience as excellent, three participants (14.3 percent) rated it as above average, six (28.5 percent) rated it as average, and none rated it as poor or below average (NASPA, 1996). The fellows praised the experience and knowledge they gained through contact with their mentors. These numbers reflect an overall positive effect of the MUFP. In a survey of former MUFP fellows from the 1989–94 classes, conducted in June 1997, 66 percent (twenty-two out of thirty-three) had received their bachelor's degree and four had received their master's degree. Several fellows indicated that they planned to pursue a master's degree or doctorate. In addition, nineteen of the thirty-three (58 percent) were employed in the field of student affairs, and 71 percent of the respondents indicated they were employed in higher education (Patitu and Terrell, 1997).

Another successful program is the NASPA Alice Manicur Symposium for women. A pilot study of the symposium was recently completed (Cynthia Jones, personal communication, Oct. 1, 1997). For the study, thirty individuals were randomly selected from past symposium participants to pilot an instrument that would be used to follow-up on all past attendees. Eighteen usable surveys were returned. Responses were tabulated using SPSS frequencies and cross-tabulations. Highlights of the results received from the pilot group are as follows: Fifty percent (n = 9) of respondents are currently Senior Student Affairs Officers (SSAOs). Thirty-three percent (n = 6) are still working toward their original SSAO goal; one individual is deferring her career goal to devote time to raising a teenager; another individual is still undecided about pursuing SSAO status as a career goal. Of the remaining respondents, only one indicated no further interest in pursuing an SSAO position. Eighty-three (n = 15) of the respondents are still at the institution listed when they attended the symposium, while 16 percent (n = 3) have moved to other institutions. Of the fifteen women still at their original institutions, six have attained SSAO status since attending the symposium (Cynthia Jones, personal communication, Oct. 1, 1997).

Prior to attending the symposium, 27 percent (n = 5) of the women were undecided about pursuing an SSAO position and 61 percent (n = 11) were clear about their plans. When asked about the effect the symposium had on their desire to pursue an SSOA position, 77 percent (n = 14) indicated that attendance confirmed their plans (eight of those who received confirmation are now SSAO's; six have not yet reached their goal but are actively in pursuit.) Eleven percent (n = 2) said that the symposium had no effect, while an additional 11 percent (n = 2) said they were still undecided following the symposium. One hundred percent of those attending indicated that they were funded by their institution. Seventy-two percent indicated they had full-institutional funding; the rest of the respondents did not clarify whether their funding was full or partial (Cynthia Jones, personal communication, Oct. 1, 1997).

When respondents were asked whether they received what they expected from the symposium, several of them commented that their confidence was built up. A few specific comments included the following:

"[It] forced me to confront real and imagined barriers and [to] grapple with my fear of failure."

"[It] encouraged me and affirmed [my] capabilities. [I am able to] share with others the frustrations of seeking such a position."

The respondents also commented on networking opportunities, support from participants, and speakers (Cynthia Jones, personal communication, Oct. 1, 1997). Clearly, this program was a success.

Conclusion

Those who have studied affirmative action's effects describe trials and failures but also triumphs in the form of substantial advances for minorities in higher education. Opponents of affirmative action might suggest that after more than three decades of civil rights legislation affirmative action is now unnecessary. In fact, "University of California Regent Ward Connerly has said this in regard to a renewed discussion about Medical School admissions policies" (Shackelford and Shackelford, 1995, p. 25).

As is evidenced by the literature and the survey responses, affirmative action has begun the process of equity in higher education. It has resulted in the establishment of many programs that promote minority student recruitment and retention. It has yet, however, to eliminate the negligible differences between the population of higher education and the community, between white versus minority participation and success. An analysis of enrollment, degree granting, and faculty employment reveals that "one, much has been achieved, and two, persons of color are far from reaching parity, and many women of all races and ethnicities continue to be underserved and underemployed" (American Council on Education, 1997). As student affairs professionals, we need to support affirmative action and its programs in order to close the gap, to ensure that opportunities are available to all, to enhance the quality of higher education institutions, and to prepare for a future that celebrates diversity.

References

Altman, E., and Promís, P. "Affirmative Action: Opportunity or Obstacle." *College and Research Libraries,* 1994, *55* (1), 11–24.

American Council on Education. *Affirmative Action: What the Research Shows.* [http://acenet.edu/Programs/DGR/AffAction/research.html]. March 13, 1997.

Astin, A. W. "Diversity and Multiculturalism on Campus: How Are Students Affected?" *Change,* 1993a, *12* (2), 44–49.

Astin, A. W. *What Matters in College? Four Critical Years Revisited.* San Francisco: Jossey-Bass, 1993b.

Borden, V.H.M. "Five-Year Trends in Minority Degree Production." *Black Issues in Higher Education,* 1996, *11* (7), 34–71.

Chahin, J. "Leadership: Diversity and the Campus Community." Paper presented at the National Conference of the American Association for Higher Education, Washington, D.C., March 1993.

Cross, T. "Suppose There Was No Affirmative Action at the Most Prestigious Colleges and Graduate Schools." *Journal of Blacks in Higher Education,* 1994a, *3,* 44–51.

Cross, T. "What If There Was No Affirmative Action in College Admissions? A Further Refinement of Our Earlier Calculations." *Journal of Blacks in Higher Education,* 1994b, *5,* 52–55.

Gomez, S. "Towards a Critical Understanding of Affirmative Action in Higher Education." [http://www.aad.berkeley.edu/95journal/SusannaGomez.html.] June 4, 1997.

Hispanic Association of Colleges and Universities. *Enhancing Quality in Higher Education: Affirmative Action and the Distribution of Resources in U.S. Department of Education Programs.* San Antonio, Tex.: Hispanic Association of Colleges and Universities, 1995.

Jones, A. C., Terrell, M. C., and Duggar, M. "The Role of Student Affairs in Fostering Cultural Diversity in Higher Education." *National Association of Student Personnel Administrators Journal,* 1991, *28* (2), 121–127.

López, G. P., Colson, E., and Schaberg, C. "An Affirmative Action Manual." [http://www.law.ucla.edu/classes/archive/civAA/bible.htm], 1996.

National Association of Student Personnel Administrators. *NASPA Minority Undergraduate Fellows Program (MUFP) 1995–96 Status Report.* Washington, D.C.: National Association of Student Personnel Administrators, 1996.

Patitu, C. L., and Terrell, M. C. "Participant Perceptions of the NASPA Minority Undergraduate Fellows Program." *College Student Affairs Journal,* 1997, *17,* 69–80.

Rockwell, P. "The Story of UCSF Affirmative Action Raises Standards: An Address on Excellence Through Diversity." *In-Motion Magazine.* [http://www.cts.com/browse/publish/rocksf.html]. May 12, 1997.

Scott, R. A. "Developing Diversity as a Campus Strength." Paper presented at the annual meeting of the Association of American Colleges, Washington D.C., Jan. 1992.

Shackelford, P. L., and Shackelford, J. F. "Affirmative Action Defended: Case Studies in Engineering Education," *Multicultural Education,* 1995, *3* (1), 25–26.

Wagner, U. *Environments of Support.* New York: Andrew W. Mellon Foundation, 1992.

CAROL LOGAN PATITU is assistant professor in the Department of Educational Administration at Texas A&M University and associate coordinator of the Student Affairs Administration in Higher Education program.

MELVIN C. TERRELL is vice president for student affairs and professor of counselor education at Northeastern Illinois University.

The Hopwood *decision has had a significant impact on student affairs in Texas. This chapter discusses strategies and guidelines for meeting the challenges created by this decision.*

A Case Study: The Effects of the *Hopwood* Decision on Student Affairs

Felicia J. Scott, William L. Kibler

Affirmative action in higher education has become one of the most contentious and hotly debated issues facing colleges and universities. The desire among university administrators, state legislators, and others to provide an environment that is equal and race-neutral while addressing the reality of increasing racial incidents on campus, growing tensions among students, and declining enrollments of ethnic minority students is forcing those in the academy to think about new paradigms. These new paradigms relate to how colleges and universities recruit and retain students of color and provide financial assistance while maintaining campus community.

For nearly twenty years, colleges and universities have relied on the 1978 Supreme Court ruling in the case of *Regents of the University of California* v. *Bakke* to develop and sustain affirmative action programs. In that case, the Supreme Court ruled that colleges could use race and ethnicity as one of many factors in admissions decisions but could not designate set numbers of spaces for members of specific ethnic and racial groups.

In the late 1970s the state of Texas was notified by the U.S. Office of Civil Rights that African Americans were segregated and Hispanics were underrepresented in student enrollment and staff at colleges and universities in Texas. Enrollment data from 1978 (see Table 5.1) show the effects of a once-dual system of higher education. Throughout this chapter, comparative data will be presented for the four largest public universities in the state (University of Texas, Texas A&M University, Texas Tech University, and the University of Houston) and for the state's two historically black institutions (Texas Southern University and Prairie View A&M University).

Table 5.1. 1978 Enrollment Figures by Ethnicity of Six Selected Universities in Texas

	Anglo	African American	Hispanic	Other
University of Houston	68 %	8.9 %	6.4 %	16.7 %
University of Texas at Austin	85	2.4	7.1	5.5
Texas A&M University	93	.6	2.0	4.4
Texas Tech University	93	1.7	2.7	2.6
Texas Southern University	1.7	74	2.7	21.6
Prairie View A&M University	4.5	94	.4	1.1

Source: Texas Higher Education Coordinating Board, 1997a.

In 1983, Texas voluntarily developed and implemented the Texas Educational Opportunity Plan for Higher Education (the Texas Plan) as a means of desegregating its higher education system. The state reviewed and submitted a revised Texas Plan in 1989. A third plan (the Access and Equity 2000 Plan) was developed and submitted in 1995 and was intended to provide guidance for taking the desegregation efforts into the next century.

During this period, the other two states in the Fifth Federal Circuit, Louisiana and Mississippi, were placed under federal court orders to desegregate their higher education systems. Other southern states that had maintained and operated dual systems of higher education, including Louisiana and Mississippi, were also placed under court order to desegregate. This distinction is important in considering the effects of the *Hopwood* decision.

Chronology of *Hopwood* v. *Texas*

As noted in Chapter Two, in recent years several court decisions have started to chip away at the precedent set in the *Bakke* case. The case *Hopwood v. Texas* (1996) began when an Anglo female named Cheryl J. Hopwood and three other applicants who were denied admission to the law school sued for reverse discrimination in 1992. Ms. Hopwood argued that she had been unfairly denied admission to the University of Texas School of Law because she was more qualified than minority applicants who had been admitted. Following are significant events during and after the case:

April 1994. The University of Texas School of Law changed its admissions process. Prior to this decision, the law school had two admissions application review panels, one for minorities and the other for everyone else.

August 1994. A U.S. district judge ruled that the plaintiffs were denied "just treatment" but they did not prove they would have been admitted even without affirmative action. Hopwood and the other litigants appealed the decision.

March 1996. A panel of the Fifth U.S. Circuit Court of Appeals reversed the district court's decision and prohibited the law school and other public higher education institutions in Texas, Louisiana, and Mississippi from considering race and ethnicity in admissions. The circuit court went on to say that a university may "properly favor one applicant over another because of his ability to play the cello, make a downfield tackle or understand chaos theory. . . . [It] may also consider an applicant's home state or relationship to school alumni" (*Hopwood* v. *Texas*, 1996, p. 961). Critics of the decision contended that the Fifth Circuit court had in essence overturned *Bakke*.

March 1996. Colleges and universities in Texas immediately halted any race-based admissions processes. Louisiana and Mississippi continued business as usual because they believed the Fifth Circuit decision did not apply to them because they were under separate federal court orders to desegregate their higher education systems.

April 1996. The Fifth Circuit court stayed the ruling, which allowed colleges and universities to consider race in admissions while the *Hopwood* decision was appealed to the U.S. Supreme Court.

July 1996. The U.S. Supreme Court decided not to hear the *Hopwood* case. Supreme Court Justice Ruth Bader Ginsburg, in a brief opinion joined by Justice David Souter, noted that the program invalidated by the appeals court "had long been abandoned by the law school." She went on to say, "we must await a final judgment on a program genuinely in controversy before addressing the important question raised in this petition." As a result, the Fifth Circuit decision in *Hopwood* became the law in the state of Texas.

August 1996. The Texas attorney general released an interpretation of the *Hopwood* decision that expanded its application beyond admissions to include financial aid and scholarships and recruitment and retention programs. The attorney general's opinion, which carries the force of law in the state, directed institutions to use only race-neutral criteria in selecting candidates for admission, financial aid and scholarships, and recruitment and retention programs and services.

January 1997. The chancellor of the University of Houston system requested an interpretation by the attorney general on the use of scholarships awarded by private companies. The attorney general reissued his stance on the use of race-neutral criteria.

January 1997. An advisory committee of the Texas Higher Education Coordinating Board suggested alternative criteria for colleges and universities to use in recruitment and retention programs. The committee predicted that using the alternative criteria would benefit only one-half of the minority students who would benefit from pre-*Hopwood* affirmative action programs.

Responses by the leadership at colleges and universities in the state varied widely. Because of the *Hopwood* decision's threat of punitive damages associated with violating the law, the most prevalent response by higher education institutions in Texas was to "cease and desist" those programs that blatantly violated *Hopwood*, such as minority-targeted scholarship programs. On many campuses, recruitment programs targeted for minority students, such as summer enrichment programs, were also halted.

A number of college presidents were outspoken about the need for diversity on college campuses and vowed to develop creative strategies to continue the progress made over the previous twenty years. The president of the University of Texas at Austin, Robert Berdahl (1996), stated that such progress was necessary because "as a flagship university, we have always educated leaders of our state and nation. We have an obligation, I believe, to prepare future leaders who reflect the diversity of the country" (p. 3).

A number of institutions formed task forces and have since partnered with former students, members of the business community, and concerned citizens to address the challenge creatively. The University of Texas Ex-Students' Association formed a scholarship program for minority students that was endorsed by the attorney general. The chancellor of the Texas Tech University System created a vice chancellor–level post focused on luring minority students and faculty—the first major public university in Texas to do so (Brooks and Roser, 1997).

Alternatively, many campus presidents chose a wait-and-see response. They articulated a continuing commitment to diversity and access but took little initiative to develop alternative responses. This inaction created an environment of uncertainty for many student affairs officers responsible for recruitment and retention programs.

Student responses to *Hopwood* were varied as well. Some hailed the decision as one that would truly make Martin Luther King Jr.'s dream of a color-blind society become reality. Their insistence that Anglo students would accept students of color based on their achievements and not on their skin color was not supported by history. Many minority students voiced concerns that they would lose their scholarships and other means of support and that their campuses would abandon efforts to continue the progress toward diversity that had been made over the last two decades. Several campuses reported growing racial tensions. Student affairs professionals were thrust into the position of trying to inform their students about the effects of *Hopwood* and to teach them what affirmative action really is. The president of Duke University, Nannerl Keohane, put these arguments in a larger context during an address at Duke's academic convocation: "You have chosen a university in the American South, [a region] with an historic legacy of slavery followed by decades of rigid segregation. The scars of that legacy won't go away easily, even as the practices themselves are changed. So race is relevant here in ways that it may not have seemed relevant in the societies from which some of you have come. . . . One of the ways it is relevant is in daily interactions and experiences in the lives of every one of you" (Keohane, 1997, p. 64).

The Texas Challenge

The *Hopwood* decision has affected Texas exclusively because the state is not under a federal court order to desegregate. More specifically, the decision has had an impact on the state's four largest public institutions: the University of

Texas, Texas A&M University, the University of Houston, and Texas Tech University. These four institutions have used selective admissions policies to manage their enrollments.

Texas has made slow progress in integrating its higher education system. The enrollment figures in Table 5.2 chronicle the state's progress prior to *Hopwood,* in 1994. In fall 1994, there were 406,466 students enrolled in four-year public universities. That enrollment was 64.2 percent Anglo, 17.6 percent Hispanic, and 8.8 percent African American. The 1990 U.S. census showed the population of Texas to be 61.6 percent Anglo, 25.6 percent Hispanic, and 11.6 percent African American (Texas Higher Education Coordinating Board, 1997a).

Population change in Texas is significant because of its impact on secondary education and, subsequently, higher education. Steve Murdock, a demographer and coauthor of the book *The Texas Challenge* (Murdock and others, 1997), notes that if current trends continue, by 2030 Texas could have a population of nearly 63 percent non-Anglos; a poorer, less well-educated population and a labor force ill prepared to compete in a global market; and substantial increases in welfare and human service usage (p. 3). These changes must be taken into account because the citizenry of the state is not being properly educated to meet the demands of the future. Kenneth Ashworth, former Texas Commissioner of Higher Education, stated that this "ruling [*Hopwood*] threatens the very diversity efforts the federal government has directed Texas to adopt. . . . Considering a future Texas' majority-minority mix, it will have a very detrimental effect" (Ackerman, 1996).

Implications

A number of statewide implications can be attributed to interpretations and reactions to *Hopwood.*

Admissions Information. Offices of admission have been and will continue to be in a state of flux in terms of admissions figures. It is important to

Table 5.2. 1994 Enrollment Figures by Ethnicity of Six Selected Universities in Texas

	Anglo	African American	Hispanic	Other
University of Houston	58 %	8.7 %	12.8 %	20.5 %
University of Texas at Austin	68	3.9	12.7	15.4
Texas A&M University	77	3	9	11
Texas Tech University	82	2.9	9.8	5.3
Texas Southern University	2.6	83	3.1	11.3
Prairie View A&M University	8.4	86	1.7	3.9

Source: Texas Higher Education Coordinating Board, 1997a.

note the differences in the number of students who apply versus those who are admitted versus those who actually enroll. Tables 5.3 and 5.4 compare the total fall class enrollment in the state by specific school. In some instances, *Hopwood* had its most staggering effect on first time enrollments (see Tables 5.5, 5.6, and 5.7).

Table 5.3. Texas Public Universities: Total Fall Class Enrollment 1996–97

	Fall 1996	Fall 1997	# Change	% Change	% of 1996 Class	% of 1997 Class
White	248,663	244,238	–4425	–2	62.59	61.51
Black	36,303	35,825	–478	–1	9.14	9.02
Hispanic	73,574	74,510	936	1	18.52	18.77
Asian/Pacific Islander	19,836	20,942	1106	6	4.99	5.27
Native American	1,931	2,011	80	4	0.49	0.51
International	16,986	17,617	631	4	4.28	4.44
Unreported	0	1,907	1,907		0.00	0.48
TOTAL	397,293	397,050	–243	0		

Source: Texas Higher Education Coordinating Board, 1997a.

Table 5.4. Selected Texas Public Universities: Total Fall Class Enrollment, 1996 vs. 1997

Fall 1996

	Texas A&M	Texas Tech	UT–Austin	U. of Houston
White	29,720	20,189	31,346	16,383
Black	1,244	729	1,911	3,173
Hispanic	3,728	2,448	6,207	4,389
Asian/Pacific Islander	1,239	411	4,989	4,618
Native American	114	101	209	158
International	2,605	839	3,346	2,053
Unreported	0	0	0	0
TOTAL	38,650	24,717	48,008	30,774

Fall 1997

	Texas A&M	Texas Tech	UT–Austin	U. of Houston
White	29,174	20,550	32,056	15,424
Black	1,166	725	1,722	3,564
Hispanic	3,666	2,429	6,105	4,692
Asian/Pacific Islander	1,211	472	5,298	4,963
Native American	136	100	230	168
International	2,615	796	3,391	2,141
Unreported	266	77	19	598
TOTAL	38,234	25,149	48,866	31,550

Source: Texas Higher Education Coordinating Board, 1997a.

Table 5.5. First-Time Freshmen Comparison,
Texas A&M University, 1996 vs. 1997

	Fall 1996	Fall 1997	# Change	% Change	% of 1996 Class	% of 1997 Class
White	5,136	5,015	–121	–2	80.41	80.46
Black	230	178	–52	–23	3.60	2.86
Hispanic	713	607	–106	–15	11.16	9.74
Asian/Pacific Islander	177	224	47	27	2.77	3.59
Native American	24	29	5	21	0.38	0.47
International	45	50	5	11	0.70	0.80
Unreported	62	130	68	110	0.97	2.09
TOTAL	6,387	6,233	–154	–2		

Source: Texas Higher Education Coordinating Board, 1997a.

Table 5.6. First-Time Freshmen Comparison,
University of Texas at Austin, 1996 vs. 1997

	Fall 1996	Fall 1997	# Change	% Change	% of 1996 Class	% of 1997 Class
White	3,657	4,461	804	66.14	66.14	67.13
Black	162	163	1	2.93	2.93	2.45
Hispanic	772	807	35	13.96	13.96	12.14
Asian/Pacific Islander	814	1,078	264	14.72	14.72	16.22
Native American	27	33	6	0.49	0.49	0.50
International	97	103	6	1.75	1.75	1.55
Unreported	0	0	0	0.00	0.00	0.00
TOTAL	5,529	6,645	20			

Source: Texas Higher Education Coordinating Board, 1997a.

Table 5.7. First-Time Freshmen Comparison,
University of Houston, 1996 vs. 1997

	Fall 1996	Fall 1997	# Change	% Change	% of 1996 Class	% of 1997 Class
White	909	1,001	92	10	37.36	34.45
Black	456	544	88	19	18.74	18.72
Hispanic	494	659	165	33	20.30	22.68
Asian/Pacific Islander	505	613	108	21	20.76	21.09
Native American	21	13	–8	–38	0.86	0.45
International	48	51	3	6	1.97	1.76
Unreported	0	25	25		0.00	0.86
TOTAL	2,433	2,906	473	19		

Source: Texas Higher Education Coordinating Board, 1997a.

Regional institutions such as the University of Houston actually benefited from *Hopwood*. University of Houston officials reported a slight increase in the number of African American and Hispanic students enrolled. The University of Houston also reported that the number of African Americans and Hispanics who applied to the university as first-time freshmen was almost the same as the number who applied in the spring of 1996 (Lum, 1997).

The decline in applications and enrolled students in Texas institutions can be attributed to a number of possible factors, including high school counselor preparation and advice, negative news media, lack of aggressive recruitment measures on the part of admissions offices, students choosing to attend college out of state, and students choosing not to attend college at all.

The challenge for admissions offices is to work collaboratively and develop relationships with underserved communities and to provide targeted recruitment programs. *Hopwood* has presented an opportunity for collaboration between the admissions office (academic affairs) and student affairs at Texas A&M University. Students, staff, and faculty have volunteered to serve as "minirecruiters" for the university at programs across the state. Furthermore, many programs in the division of student affairs have been reviewed as possible ways to recruit students on a more formal basis. An example is the Minority Enrichment and Development through Academic and Leadership Skills program that brings together several hundred minority students from across the state for a two-day program designed to encourage them to go to college. This is one example of how one student affairs division has collaborated with academic affairs to enhance recruitment.

Scholarships and Financial Aid. When the Texas attorney general declared that scholarships and financial aid were part of the *Hopwood* decision, the outlook for increasing the number of students of color in Texas colleges and universities was bleak. Texas A&M University and the University of Texas at Austin had both historically utilized funds from the Available University Fund (an endowment fund from oil and gas revenues) for merit-based competitive scholarships for African American and Hispanic students. Although these funds were a small portion of the overall scholarship budgets at both institutions, they had been used quite successfully to attract the best and the brightest minority students in the state. Once *Hopwood* was affirmed, the honors and scholarship office at Texas A&M University responded by combining this targeted money with the general scholarship fund and awarding scholarships based on race-neutral criteria. A minimum standardized test score was required to enter the competition; then other factors such as leadership, essays, and letters of recommendation were considered. Officials in the honors and scholarship office reported that there was a significant decline in the number of scholarship applications received from African Americans and Hispanics in 1996–97. As a result, Texas A&M University's scholarship offers to Anglo students in 1996–97 rose by 28 percent, while offers to Hispanic students declined by 60 percent and offers to African American students were down by 76 percent. It must be noted, however, that the overall number of scholarship offers dropped 28 percent from 1995–96 to 1996–97 (Honors Programs and Academic Scholarship Office, 1997).

Offices of student financial aid have more flexibility than merit-based scholarship offices because of their ability to award funds on the basis of need rather than merit. Using this process has yielded a better cross-section of races than merit-based programs alone, which tended to rely heavily on standardized test scores. A concern expressed by administrators of merit-based scholarship programs is, If eligible funds are used for need-based scholarships or financial aid, will the overall quality of students drop? This concern is causing institutions to reconsider how quality is defined and to focus on the issue of colleges and universities partnering with K–12 schools to better prepare students for success in higher education.

Precollege Programs. Precollege and summer enrichment programs targeted for underrepresented groups have proven to be excellent opportunities to improve access to college while enhancing skill development. As a result of *Hopwood,* many of these programs have been altered to be all-inclusive or they have been discontinued entirely.

At the University of Texas at Austin, the Preview Program, a summer bridge program for African American and Hispanic students, was altered to include all students. Many supporters of the tenets of the *Hopwood* case suggest that programs such as Preview should be open to all students. The concern of program administrators is whether a race-neutral program will benefit all parties or eventually become race-specific for Anglos.

Outreach programs such as the Exploring Leadership Opportunities and Rewards in Education program at Texas A&M University for minority students interested in careers in education altered the criteria for selection by requesting students who have an interest in teaching in inner-city and diverse settings. This is a legal selection criteria that does not serve as a substitute for race. In this instance, program planners are maintaining the integrity of the program while staying within the guidelines of the law.

Federally funded precollege programs are also in jeopardy. Camp Planet Earth, funded by the National Science Foundation (NSF) and the National Institute of Health (NIH) Minority High School Student Research Apprenticeship were two programs at Texas A&M University that came under fire as a result of *Hopwood.* Camp Planet Earth was an outreach program designed to encourage seventh and eighth grade minority students to pursue careers in the geosciences. Jane Doe, an Anglo female, applied and was admitted to the program; university officials rescinded the offer, however, when they realized that she was not one of the targeted ethnic groups dictated by NSF. When the student and her family filed suit, the NSF settled out of court and canceled the program, leaving Texas A&M University with no alternative but to settle as well.

In the case of the NIH program, the same Jane Doe sued the university and the parties involved. Although this lawsuit has not been settled to date, the major difference is that program officials had already changed the criteria for the program, so Jane Doe would likely have been selected if she had applied.

Litigation against programs such as the ones described in this chapter are being settled out of court because of the fear of having them go to the federal courts and establish a precedent. A number of federal and private funds that are specifically targeted for minority students are in jeopardy or have been eliminated. Unfortunately, the equipment, staff, and other material benefits from such funds are lost by the institutions, and the general society does not benefit from the preparation of the affected students through these programs to be productive citizens.

State Response. Texas lawmakers responded to the *Hopwood* challenge by passing a law that guarantees automatic admission to state universities for Texas high school seniors who graduate in the top 10 percent of their classes regardless of college entrance exam scores or high school curricula. The intent was to "assure college slots for high performing students at largely minority high schools" (Moreno, 1997, p. 33a).

The implications of this legislation for admissions at selective colleges and universities is unknown, because the first class to be admitted under this requirement will be in the fall of 1998. If 10 percent of all graduating high school students in Texas apply to enter public institutions in fall 1998, there will be a pool of sixteen thousand freshmen who must be admitted without regard for other qualifications (Texas Higher Education Coordinating Board, 1997a). This situation would create a potential challenge for admissions offices at selective public institutions to consider how to allocate the remaining spaces in the entering classes. Another challenge is that admissions offices have no historical data on the percentage of these students who will actually enroll; thus it will be very difficult for these institutions to project how many students to admit to hit their desired enrollment numbers.

Retention concerns at all public institutions are also heightened by the 10 percent admissions criteria. Without specific course requirements, a student in the top 10 percent could be ill prepared for the college experience. The 10 percent plan provides a challenge and an opportunity at institutions across the state for student affairs to work collaboratively with academic affairs on bridge-type programs, financial aid packages, and other areas of retention.

The Texas Higher Education Coordinating Board formed a statewide advisory committee to study and identify race-neutral alternative criteria that would maintain diversity on campuses. They identified and recommended the following ten factors: socioeconomic background; first-generation college status; bilingual proficiency; financial status of the student's school district; performance level of the student's school; student responsibilities; region of residence within the state of Texas; residence within rural or urban, central city or suburban areas of the state; effects of the use of alternative levels of ACT and SAT scores; and student ACT and SAT rankings within socioeconomic levels (Texas Higher Education Coordinating Board, 1997b). Although use of these criteria would yield some level of diversity in college admissions, the authors of the committee's report pointed out that the best way to maintain racial diversity is the use of race as one of the determinants. Furthermore, there is not enough empirical evidence on the cultural characteristics or socioeconomic realities of life for African Americans and Hispanics in Texas to accurately predict the outcome of using these criteria. What is clear is that "public schools have not provided a quality education for minorities and have not prepared them for higher education. . . . Their cultural capital has been lost in a number of educational settings from public schools to colleges and universities" (Texas Higher Education Coordinating Board, 1997b, p. 32).

Portales (1997) summarizes the overall challenge faced by the state of Texas in addressing the effects of Hopwood: "The main solution in the wake of *Hopwood* is to repair the educational pipeline from K–12, providing more minority students with a higher quality education so that they are eligible to apply successfully to the very competitive, the highly competitive and the most competitive colleges and universities. Despite efforts in this direction, K–12 schools in Texas, California, and everywhere else in the United States are not now accomplishing this desired and needed goal" (p. 10).

In response to the effects of Proposition 209 in California (a precursor to *Hopwood*), the University of California system recommended a three-point strategy that has implications for student affairs: school-centered partnerships, academic development, and informational outreach (Portales, 1997, p. 10).These strategies are simple; however, student affairs and academic affairs need to ensure that the "turf wars" that often exist between their divisions do not prevent them from coming together to determine effective ways to address the challenges presented by *Hopwood*. There are important issues for student affairs practitioners to consider when planning programs and services in this environment.

Checklist for Student Affairs

Sixteen fundamental principles from the Council for the Advancement of Standards, which serves as one measure of the effectiveness of student affairs programs, include the following (Miller, 1997, pp. 7–8):

3. Each student is a unique person and must be treated as such. . . .
5. The student's total environment is educational and must be used to achieve full individual development. . . .
6. Institutions of higher learning reflect the diversity of the societies and cultures in which they exist; they are intended to guide, instruct, and educate today's youth to be tomorrow's leaders, and to provide opportunities for lifelong learning to all. . . .
10. Recognizing the nature of racial and ethnic diversity on campuses, student support programs and services are committed to eliminating barriers that impede student learning and development, paying special attention to establishing and maintaining diverse human relationships essential to survival in today's global society. . . .

Student affairs practitioners have a role and responsibility in preparing students for a multicultural environment. Legal mandates such as *Hopwood,* Proposition 209, and others that will come should cause us to refocus and assess our programs and services to ensure that they are living up to our mission and purpose.

The issues and arguments surrounding the *Hopwood* case and other affir- mative action cases are of extreme importance to student affairs practitioners. Many of the programs affected are operated by student affairs divisions. Recruitment and retention programs that have been in place must be assessed and reviewed to ensure compliance with the strict scrutiny and narrowly tailored legal concepts discussed in *Hopwood* and similar cases. Programs and services that historically have been designed for specific groups may need to be modified to maintain the integrity of the program.

Student affairs should take the lead in continuing to build community and in being proactive in anticipation of these changes affecting other parts of the country. The *Hopwood* decision and subsequent interpretations by the attorney general caused turmoil in many institutions because they did not effectively anticipate the legal and political environment. Communication with all affected parties is an essential key to coping successfully with the aftermath of these changes. Committees and task forces that are formed should be representative of major units in order for the institution to be able to respond consistently. Top-level administrators should ensure that communication regarding issues such as this are communicated clearly, openly, and often. Many Texas administrators failed to understand why students did not understand the institution's stance on diversity. Many students were operating on hearsay information due to the legal and political nature of the issues, and because discussions about *Hopwood* were held behind closed doors and did not involve students. Involving students and practitioners is key when making decisions to modify or eliminate programs, because students have firsthand information on the anticipated impact of such changes. Furthermore, involving a number of groups campuswide helps to eliminate the problem of misinformation. For example, a common misperception by students who were recipients of minority scholarships was that they would lose all their scholarship funds because of *Hopwood.* Such dissonance in communication causes confusion and the institution is seen as an uncaring entity.

Programs that have been operated because they are the "right thing to do" may not hold up in a court of law. It therefore behooves student affairs practitioners to begin formalizing assessment processes and procedures that provide justification and accountability for programs that are easy targets.

In summary, student affairs practitioners should adhere to three basic and traditional principles: communicate, collaborate, and change. Student affairs has the opportunity to take the lead on two issues that have been thrust to the forefront in Texas by *Hopwood*—access and inclusion. These values, along with openness, fairness, and opportunity, will provide an avenue for discussion for years to come.

Court Cases Cited

Regents of the University of California v. *Bakke*, 438 U.S. 265 (1978).
Hopwood v. *Texas*, 78 F.3d 932 (5th Cir. 1996).

References

Ackerman, T. "Harmful Effect Seen in Ruling on UT Lawsuit." *Houston Chronicle,* Mar. 21, 1996, pp. 1A, 18A.

Berdahl, R. "Understanding *Hopwood:* The University's President Considers Race and Education." *Texas Alcade,* 1996, *84* (6). [http://www.utexas.edu/alumni/alcade/hopwood.html].

Brooks, A., and Roser, M. "Colleges Try Different Tacks for Diversity." *Austin American Statesman,* Sept. 2, 1997, pp. A1, A6.

Honors Programs and Academic Scholarships Office. Scholarship offers and acceptances. Unpublished raw data. College Station: Texas A&M University, 1997.

Keohane, N. "The Relevance of Race." *Black Issues in Higher Education,* 1997, *14,* 64.

Lum, L. "College Numbers for Hispanics, Blacks Edge Up." *Houston Chronicle,* Mar. 19, 1997, p. 1A.

Miller, T. K. (ed.). *The Book of Professional Standards for Higher Education.* Washington, D.C.: Council for the Advancement of Standards in Higher Education, 1997.

Moreno, S. "Senate OKs Bill on College Admissions." *The Dallas Morning News,* Apr. 11, 1997, pp. 33A, 38A.

Murdock, S., Hoque, M., Michael, M., White, S., and Pecotte, B. *The Texas Challenge: Population Change and the Future of Texas.* College Station: Texas A&M University Press, 1997.

Portales, M. "Admissions Policies, Institutional Rankings and Eligible Minority Students." Unpublished manuscript, 1997.

Texas Higher Education Coordinating Board, Committee on Access and Equity. *Entering Class Enrollment Data, 1996 v. 1997.* Austin, Tex.: Texas Higher Education Coordinating Board Committee on Access and Equity, 1997a.

Texas Higher Education Coordinating Board. *Alternative Diversity Criteria: Analysis and Recommendations.* Austin, Tex.: Texas Higher Education Coordinating Board, 1997b.

FELICIA J. SCOTT *currently serves as assistant to the vice president for student affairs and is completing her doctoral studies in educational administration at Texas A&M University.*

WILLIAM L. KIBLER *is associate vice president for student affairs and associate professor of educational administration at Texas A&M University.*

Cultural diversity on campus need not suffer if affirmative action is dismantled. This chapter offers alternative approaches to achieve this desirable institutional goal.

Recommendations for the Future

Bettina C. Shuford

Is thirty years of affirmative action enough? The answer to this question is being debated in public institutions across the country. Affirmative action was first introduced in 1961 by President John F. Kennedy in Executive Order 10925 as a mechanism for ending discrimination in government employment and contracting. The executive order requested that contractors should take "affirmative action" to ensure the fair treatment of employees regardless of their race, creed, color, or national origin. Four years later, President Lyndon Johnson issued Executive Order 11246, mandating "equal opportunity in Federal employment for qualified persons, to prohibit discrimination in employment because of race, creed, color, or national origin, and to promote the full realization of equal employment opportunity through a positive, continuing program in each executive department and agency" (3 C.F.R. 339).

More than thirty years later, some Americans are questioning whether affirmative action has outlived its purpose or whether it has reached the goals it set out to achieve. The answers to these questions have become an interesting dilemma for many in the higher education community. The quest to find the answers is even more perplexing because when it was first introduced in the early 1960s no goals were set for what affirmative action should look like (Tierney, 1997). As a result, there is no gauge to determine the success or failure of affirmative action.

Judicial Tide

Amid criticism that affirmative action discriminates against groups not protected by the policy, that it victimizes the groups that it was created to serve, and that it dilutes standards by hiring and admitting individuals who are less qualified than their white male counterparts, there are those who believe that affirmative action has benefitted American society. Despite the debates for and against affirmative action, recent decisions by the courts have significantly influenced its future. The first case to affect the future of affirmative action was a Fifth Circuit ruling that struck down the use of race in admissions decisions at the University of Texas Law School (*Hopwood v. State of Texas,* 1996). In essence, this case overruled a long-standing precedent set in the *Regents of the University of California v. Bakke* (1978) case, which determined that race could serve as a plus factor in admissions decisions. The Fifth Circuit's decision applies only to institutions in Texas, Louisiana, and Mississippi. So, *Bakke* is still good case law for the rest of the country. However, as Alan Kolling points out in Chapter Two, the challenge may come not from the federal courts but rather from the state legislatures.

The first legislative action to affect the future of affirmative action was the passing in the November 1996 election of Proposition 209 to amend California's constitution. Proposition 209 bans the use of affirmative action in hiring, admission, and contracting decisions in programs mandated by the state (Bensimon and Soto, 1997; "Results of State Referenda . . .," 1996).

As a result of the recent bans on affirmative action in California and the Fifth Circuit decision, some institutions have reaffirmed their commitment to affirmative action while others have begun to readdress race-based admission policies and scholarships. For instance, institutions in Arkansas, Michigan, and Wisconsin have begun to review affirmative action policies on their campuses (Caplan, Friedman, and Barnes, 1996). A class-action lawsuit was recently filed by eleven black and white plaintiffs against the University of Georgia system, questioning the use of race in admissions and hiring decisions (Rankin, 1997). This suit could have a detrimental effect on the legitimacy of the state's three historically black institutions. Historically black institutions are by their very existence discriminatory in that race is an identifiable characteristic of the institution (Healy, 1997). If the plaintiffs prevail in this case, the special mission of the historically black college to provide greater access to higher education for black Americans will be eliminated.

Support for Affirmative Action from the Higher Education Community

Despite the attacks on affirmative action, there is still much support for it in the higher education community. The American Council on Education, in conjunction with twenty-two other higher education associations sent a letter on September 13, 1995, to college presidents, signifying their continued support for affirmative action. In the letter, the associations stated that affirmative action is "a useful and important tool that helps colleges and universities achieve the goals of equal opportunity, educational quality, diversity, and inclusion" (American Council on Education, 1995). The National Association of Student Personnel Administrators (NASPA) was one of the undersigned associations that lent support for affirmative action.

Effect of Diversity on College Students

As noted in the American Council on Education's letter, there is support for affirmative action because of the perceived contribution it makes to diversity on college campuses. As Patitu and Terrell observed in their chapter in this volume (Chapter Four), there is support in the literature that a diverse student population has a positive effect on the campus community. Research findings also support this contention (Astin, 1993; Pascarella and others, 1996). Astin (1993) examined the impact of college on student outcomes over a four-year period with 24,847 students from 217 different institutions and found that students from all racial and ethnic backgrounds benefit from institutions that have a visible commitment to diversity. Initiatives such as institutional goals or commitment to policies to increase minorities in the student population and minorities and women on the faculty, and an emphasis on multiculturalism, positively affected student's self-reported growth in cultural awareness and their commitment to the goal of racial understanding. They also had a positive effect on satisfaction with student life and the overall college experience. Participating in discussions about racial or ethnic issues had a positive effect on students' critical thinking abilities, analytical and problem solving skills, and writing skills. The inclusion of students from diverse populations and backgrounds provides opportunities for students to hear a variety of perspectives about race and ethnic issues. In turn, exposure to diverse perspectives enhances the cognitive development of students. Astin's research lends support for the need to have a campus population that is diverse and committed to multicultural issues.

Similar findings on the impact of diversity on college campuses were reported by Pascarella and his colleagues (1996) in a three-year longitudinal study with 3,840 students. A nondiscriminatory racial environment at the institution, on-campus residence, participation in cultural awareness workshops, and extent of involvement with diverse student peers had a significant positive impact on students' end-of-the-year openness to diversity and challenge. White students who were more open to diversity at the beginning of their first year had more culturally diverse interactions and participated in discussions on race and ethnicity more frequently than students who were initially less open. By the end of the first year, the white students who were initially more open to diverse perspectives had perceptions about prejudice against minority students that were similar to the perceptions of students of color. These results have significant implications for student affairs practitioners. Because we know the impact that peer influence has on learning, student affairs practitioners should be intentionally creating opportunities for students of diverse backgrounds to interact with one another on an ongoing basis.

Alternatives to Affirmative Action

Although the tide is turning against the use of race in hiring and admissions decisions in higher education, the higher education community is still interested in maintaining racial diversity on its campuses. If affirmative action as we know it is dismantled, how are institutions to achieve a diverse student body and faculty while still complying with the law?

D'Souza (1996) describes four basic policy options for addressing racial preference: equal representation in the workforce that is proportional to the surrounding population; elimination of racial preferences for all groups except African Americans because of their unique history in the United States; a nondiscrimination rule that shows no preference due to race in both the private and public sector (socioeconomic affirmative action is permissible in this model); and elimination of racial preferences in employment and admissions in the public sector only. In the latter approach, the government is held to a "rigorous standard of race neutrality", while the private sector is allowed to consider race in hiring decisions (D'Souza, 1996, p. 28). Of course, such a provision would require the Civil Rights Act of 1964 to be modified to apply "only to the government and those businesses truly offering 'public accommodation,' such as hotels and large retail establishments" (D'Souza, 1996, p. 30). Proposition 209 and the *Hopwood* case (1996) similarly apply to public venues.

As Bickel suggested in Chapter One of this volume, there is another method for addressing the elimination of affirmative action—redefining the definition of merit. There are many in the academy who support this option, particularly eliminating the use of standardized test in admissions decisions (Sturm and Guinier, 1996; Tierney, 1997). Nearly half of all the institutions in higher education use some form of standardized measure in their admissions decisions (Crouse and Trusheim, 1991). Standardized tests such as the SAT are used to predict academic success in the first year of college. Through an examination of the regression formulas used to predict GPA, Crouse and Trusheim found that there was very little difference in estimates of predicted success between using combined high school records with SAT scores and using high school records alone. When Crouse and Trusheim (1988) looked at the effect that SAT scores have on black applicants, they found that the SAT score has a much more negative effect on black applicants than on white applicants. According to Crouse and Trusheim (1988), their research indicated "that when admissions decisions are made without regard to applicants' color—so that the same standards are used for whites and blacks—adding the SAT to the high school record reduces the number of blacks admitted to colleges, sometimes by more than half, but does not reduce the number of whites admitted" (p. 103).

There are other attributes, such as motivation and creativity, that are not as easy to measure as what the SAT measures but that may be better predictors of academic success than one's ability to take a standardized test (Sturm and Guinier, 1996). Rather than using standardized tests as a form of meritocracy in employment and admissions decisions, institutions should evaluate the attributes they deem important in employment and admissions decisions (Sturm and Guinier, 1996). A one-size-fits-all standard for measuring future performance may not be the best method for admitting students.

The University of Texas Regents are now using new criteria in their admissions decisions. Letters of reference; performance in challenging course work;

and background, leadership, and academic interests of students as described in an essay are all considered in the admissions decision (Marchese, 1996). UC-Irvine also looks at variables other than academic achievement to help them select a diverse student body. They use a personal profile review that looks at leadership and initiative, honors and awards, geographic challenges, personal challenges, self-awareness, civic and cultural awareness, and specialized knowledge (Fields, 1997).

As Pavela suggested in Chapter Three of this volume, affirmative action based on caste might be preferable to race-based programs. There has in fact been a push by some in the academy to substitute race-based affirmative action with a class-based formula (Luney, 1996). Social class was also listed in the *Bakke* case as one of many factors that could be used in admissions decisions (1978). A class-based affirmative action policy, however, would be applicable only in admissions decisions. Luney (1996) argued that it would be difficult to show how one's socioeconomic background could benefit campus diversity in hiring decisions.

Another alternative to affirmative action is equalizing the playing field by providing greater academic support to students prior to their matriculation into higher education. Early and sustained intervention at the secondary level should increase the college going rate of underrepresented students, thus eliminating the need for affirmative action (Marchese, 1996). The following quote captures the essence of the need for an early intervention model: "If we do affirmative action in grade 3, we won't have to do it in grade 13" (Gladieux, 1996, p. 8). Students of color make up 60 percent of the students who are currently participating in precollege programs (Gladieux, 1996). Upward Bound and Educational Talent Search programs have been quite successful at preparing low-income, first-generation students for postsecondary education. A number of universities and colleges have offered precollege programs as a mechanism for getting underrepresented students through the pipeline to higher education. Adelman (1997) affirmed that early intervention programs rather than the use of race as a criterion in admissions decisions should be the primary method for diversifying college campuses. He recommended that the higher education community should significantly increase the number of college outreach programs in the next five years. Students should begin these programs while they are still in middle school and should be equipped with a computer and access to the Internet within the program.

A slightly different way of approaching affirmative action than as just a means to increasing numbers on campus is to focus on diversity as an educational outcome. Lyons (1997) argued that racial preference in admissions decisions should be used as a mechanism to improve the educational mission of an institution and not as reparation for past discrimination. With this method the requirements for admission are determined at the institutional level. Race-based considerations are used not as a mechanism for correcting past discrimination but as a future orientation in which diversity as an educational outcome benefits all students. Individuals who enhance the diversity for a particular campus are admitted (Cahn, 1997). For instance, a histori-cally black institution might be enhanced by the preferential admission of a white student, or a predominantly Irish American college might benefit from the preferential admission of a Middle Eastern student (Lyons, 1997). The cat-egories used in affirmative action are expanded to meet institutional needs. The individuals in this case are selected not because they are deficient (due to past discrimination) but because the larger campus population is deficient in diversity. The campus is enhanced as a result of bringing in diverse stu-dents, faculty, and staff (Cahn, 1997).

Implications for Student Affairs

Diversity as an educational outcome has significant implications for student affairs. Whether affirmative action remains a viable force or not, student affairs has an obligation to help students become culturally competent citizens in a global society. The Workforce 2000 report (Johnston and Packer, 1987) predicted that 80 percent of the individuals going into the workforce by the year 2000 will be women, persons of color, and recent immigrants. Higher education and stu-dent affairs must prepare students to be able to function in such a diverse work setting. It is imperative for a college-educated person in this day and age to have some knowledge about other cultures (Bok, 1986; Bowen, 1977; Rosovski, 1990). In addition, students must value and appreciate diverse perspectives.

Student affairs practitioners should work with their colleagues in acade-mic affairs to provide a holistic approach to multicultural education (Howard-Hamilton, Richardson, and Shuford, in press). Faculty, staff, and administrators must dialogue to determine what knowledge, skills, and attitudes students should possess to be culturally competent. The curriculum, programs, and activities should be structured in such a manner to develop and enhance each cultural competency.

Student affairs practitioners must also create opportunities for sustained interaction between diverse student populations. A true understanding of diversity cannot come from textbooks alone. Students need to engage in dis-cussions about multicultural issues. They must seek out opportunities for direct interaction with other cultures. The programs and services in student affairs must be inclusive of diverse perspectives and must structure in oppor-tunities for students to come together and dialogue about cultural differences as well as about the commonalities that cultural groups share.

Student affairs must also work to help create a campus environment that values diversity. The Carolina creed at the University of South Carolina sends a strong statement to students, faculty, and staff that the institution values a campus culture that promotes civility, compassion, empathy, and openness to diverse perspectives (Pruitt, 1996). There is no question as to what the uni-versity's stance is about diversity or what behaviors and attitudes will be toler-ated in the community.

Student affairs practitioners should lend support to college outreach pro-grams for underrepresented students that are sponsored by their institution. If such a program does not exist, they should work to create one. Student affairs practitioners can serve as mentors to these students. They can provide opportunities for students to participate in cultural activities on campus during the academic year, and they can provide accommodations for living-learning opportunities in the summer. Such efforts will increase the college's going rate of underrepresented students.

Efforts should also be made to diversify the candidate pool of individuals going into the student affairs profession. Programs such as those mentioned by Patitu and Terrell in their chapter, including NASPA's Minority Undergraduate Fellows Program, help to increase the pool of potential candidates for the student affairs profession by identifying students of color who have potential for graduate school and providing them with opportunities to be mentored by seasoned practitioners in the profession. NASPA realized that if it wanted a diverse workforce, it had to identify students early on in their undergraduate careers who had the potential to make good student affairs practitioners, and it had to provide them with learning experiences and opportunities for success in the profession.

Conclusion

A number of options have been provided throughout this monograph and in this chapter on ways to diversify the higher education community. If affirmative action is dismantled, it will certainly make our job of maintaining a multicultural campus environment much harder. The momentum gained in the last decade, however, does not have to be lost if institutions move away from one-size-fit-all standards for measuring future performance. Applying color-blind criteria in a society that does not operate in a color-blind manner is not a fair and equitable method. Measures of achievement, such as SAT scores, need to be reevaluated as to whether they are effective in measuring academic success in higher education.

Efforts to achieve diversity in higher education must begin earlier in students' academic careers. We can no longer wait until students are ready to matriculate into higher education to address past inequities. Interventions to correct past injustices must begin at the elementary and intermediate levels. If students of color are better prepared at the secondary level, their quest to enter higher education will no longer be circumspect. Students of all races will be similarly qualified and judgments will be made in a fair and equitable manner.

What the future holds for affirmative action is still up for debate. Recent constitutional revisions and case law do not support the continuation of affirmative action. Diversity does not have to suffer, however, because affirmative action is no longer in place. If institutions are committed to diversity, they will find ways to continue to diversify their campus populations.

Court Cases Cited

Hopwood v. *State of Texas*, 78 F.3d. 932 (5th Cir. 1996).
Regents of the University of California v. *Bakke*, 438 U.S. 265 (1978).

References

Adelman, C. "Diversity: Walk the Walk, and Drop the Talk." *Change,* July/Aug. 1997, pp. 34–45.

American Council on Education, "Joint Association Letter on Affirmative Action." Letter to college presidents in support of affirmative action. American Council on Education, Washington, D.C., Sept. 13, 1995.

Astin, A. *What Matters in College? Four Critical Years Revisited.* San Francisco: Jossey-Bass, 1993.

Bensimon, E. M., and Soto, M. "Can We Rebuild Civic Life Without a Multicultural University?" *Change,* Jan./Feb. 1997, pp. 42–44.

Bok, D. C. *Higher Learning.* Cambridge, Mass.: Harvard University Press, 1986.

Bowen, H. *Investment in Learning.* San Francisco: Jossey-Bass, 1977.

Cahn, S. M. "Two Concepts of Affirmative Action." *Academe,* Jan.–Feb. 1997, pp. 14–19.

Caplan, L., Friedman, D., and Barnes, J. "The *Hopwood* Effect Kicks in on Campus." *U.S. News and World Report,* Dec. 23, 1996, pp. 26–28.

Crouse, J., and Trusheim, D. "The Case Against the SAT." *Public Interest,* 1988, *93,* 97–110.

Crouse, J., and Trusheim, D. "How Colleges Can Correctly Determine Selection Benefits from the SAT." *Harvard Educational Review,* 1991, *61* (2), 125–147.

D'Souza, D. "Beyond Affirmative Action." *National Review,* Dec. 9, 1996, pp. 26–30.

Fields, C. D. "Harvard Scholars Convene Civil Rights Think Tank." *Black Issues in Higher Education,* May 1, 1997, pp. 8–11.

Gladieux, L. "A Diverse Student Body: The Challenge of Equalizing College Opportunities." *The Journal of College Admissions,* 1996, *152–153,* 4–9.

Healy, P. "Civil-Rights Groups Seek to Intervene in Georgia Suit on Affirmative Action." *The Chronicle of Higher Education,* July 3, 1997, p. A32.

Howard-Hamilton, M., Richardson, B., and Shuford, B. "Promoting Multicultural Education: A Holistic Approach." *College Student Affairs Journal,* in press.

Johnston, W. B., and Packer, A. E. *Workforce 2000: Work and Workers for the Twenty-First Century.* Indianapolis, Ind.: Hudson Institute, 1987.

Luney, P. R. "Affirmative Action: Forgoing a Constitutionally Acceptable Solution." *Black Issues in Higher Education,* May 30, 1996, pp. 30–31.

Lyons, J. "Racial and Ethnic Preferences: A New Era." *Academe,* Jan./Feb., 1997, 12–13.

Marchese, T. "After *Hopwood.*" *Change,* Sept./Oct. 1996, 4.

Pascarella, E. T., Whitt, E. J., Nora, A., Edison, M., Hagedom, L. S., and Terenzini, P. T. "What Have We Learned from the First Year of the National Study of Student Learning?" *Journal of College Student Development,* 1996, *37* (2), 182–192.

Pruitt, D. A. "In Practice: The Carolina Creed." *About Campus,* 1996, *1* (2), 27–29.

Rankin, B. "Suit Rattles State Colleges: Race-Based Preferences in Hiring, Admissions Attacked." *Atlanta Constitution,* Mar. 4, 1997, p. 1.

"Results of State Referenda Affecting Colleges." *The Chronicle of Higher Education,* Nov. 15, 1996, p. 142.

Rosovski, H. *The University: An Owner's Manual.* New York: Norton, 1990.

Sturm, S., and Guinier, L. "The Future of Affirmative Action: Reclaiming the Innovative Ideal." *California Law Review,* 1996, *84* (4), 953–1036.

Tierney, W. G. "The Parameters of Affirmative Action: Equity and Excellence in the Academy." *Review of Educational Research,* 1997, *67* (2), 165–196.

BETTINA C. SHUFORD *is the program assistant for College Access Programs and Multicultural Affairs at Bowling Green State University and a doctoral student at Bowling Green State University.*

INDEX

Back Issue/Subscription Order Form

Copy or detach and send to:
Jossey-Bass Inc., Publishers, 350 Sansome Street, San Francisco CA 94104-1342

Call or fax toll free!
Phone 888-378-2537 6AM-5PM PST; Fax 800-605-2665

Back issues:　　Please send me the following issues at $23 each
(Important: please include series initials and issue number, such as SS90)

1. SS _____

_____

_____

$ _____ Total for single issues

$ _____ Shipping charges (for single issues *only;* subscriptions are exempt
from shipping charges): Up to $30, add $5^{50} • $30^{01}–$50, add $6^{50}
$50^{01}–$75, add $7^{50} • $75^{01}–$100, add $9 • $100^{01}–$150, add $10
Over $150, call for shipping charge

Subscriptions　　Please ❑ start　❑ renew my subscription to *New Directions
for Student Services* for the year 19___ at the following rate:

❑ Individual $56　　❑ Institutional $99
NOTE: Subscriptions are quarterly, and are for the calendar year only.
Subscriptions begin with the spring issue of the year indicated above.
For shipping outside the U.S., please add $25.

$ _____ Total single issues and subscriptions (CA, IN, NJ, NY and DC
residents, add sales tax for single issues. NY and DC residents must
include shipping charges when calculating sales tax. NY and Canadian
residents only, add sales tax for subscriptions.)

❑ Payment enclosed (U.S. check or money order only)

❑ VISA, MC, AmEx, Discover Card # _____ Exp. date _____

Signature _____ Day phone _____

❑ Bill me (U.S. institutional orders only. Purchase order required.)

Purchase order # _____

Name _____

Address _____

_____

Phone _____ E-mail _____

For more information about Jossey-Bass Publishers, visit our Web site at:
www.josseybass.com　　　　　　　　　**PRIORITY CODE = ND1**

OTHER TITLES AVAILABLE IN THE
NEW DIRECTIONS FOR STUDENT SERVICES SERIES
John H. Schuh, Editor-in-Chief
Elizabeth J. Whitt, Associate Editor